Exploring Communi
Further and Adult Ec

Drawing on international research and professional practice, this book provides a rich, detailed, and accessible guide to Communities of Practice (CoP) theory, with information on how the theory is constructed, the research that it rests on, and the ways that it has been used in thinking about learning and teaching in the further and adult education sectors.

Exploring Communities of Practice in Further and Adult Education introduces CoP theory and the theory of learning that goes with it. It provides empirical examples of CoP research from a range of settings, including further and adult education, to illustrate how CoPs form and work within educational settings, including thinking about assessment and evaluation. It also explores how different CoPs work together and can learn from each other. With these key elements described, this book demonstrates how CoPs can be used in further and adult education settings to help understand more about how students and staff learn.

With engaging material including examples from research, prompts for professional learning, and case studies, this comprehensive and accessible title will appeal to student teachers and beginning teachers as well as more experienced teachers in the sector looking to refresh their practice.

Jonathan Tummons is Professor in the School of Education at Durham University, UK.

Exploring Communities of Practice in Further and Adult Education

Apprenticeship, Expertise and Belonging

Jonathan Tummons

Routledge
Taylor & Francis Group

LONDON AND NEW YORK

Cover image: © Getty Images

First published 2023
by Routledge
4 Park Square, Milton Park, Abingdon, Oxon OX14 4RN

and by Routledge
605 Third Avenue, New York, NY 10158

Routledge is an imprint of the Taylor & Francis Group, an informa business

© 2023 Jonathan Tummons

The right of Jonathan Tummons to be identified as author of this work has been asserted in accordance with sections 77 and 78 of the Copyright, Designs and Patents Act 1988.

British Library Cataloguing-in-Publication Data
A catalogue record for this book is available from the British Library

Library of Congress Cataloging-in-Publication Data
Names: Tummons, Jonathan, author.
Title: Exploring communities of practice in further and adult education : apprenticeship, expertise and belonging / Jonathan Tummons.
Identifiers: LCCN 2022037646 (print) | LCCN 2022037647 (ebook) |
ISBN 9781032180311 (Hardback) | ISBN 9781032180335 (Paperback) |
ISBN 9781003252566 (eBook)
Subjects: LCSH: Communities of practice. | Adult learning. | Adult education. | Continuing education.
Classification: LCC LB1707 .T86 2023 (print) | LCC LB1707 (ebook) |
DDC 374/.22--dc23/eng/20220831
LC record available at https://lccn.loc.gov/2022037646
LC ebook record available at https://lccn.loc.gov/2022037647

ISBN: 978-1-032-18031-1 (hbk)
ISBN: 978-1-032-18033-5 (pbk)
ISBN: 978-1-003-25256-6 (ebk)

DOI: 10.4324/9781003252566

Typeset in Bembo
by Taylor & Francis Books

Contents

Acknowledgements

Thanks to my Durham University friends/colleagues for being superb at being both friends and colleagues: Oakleigh Welply; Rille Raaper; Cristina Costa; Anna Llewellyn; Laura Mazzoli Smith; Dimitra Kokotsaki; Julie Rattray.

Thanks to my Oxford Ethnography and Education Conference friends/colleagues as well, for the same reasons: Lisa Russell; Shari Sabeti; Ruth Barley; Courtney Stafford-Walter; Marilyn Blake.

Thanks are also due to two people in particular who have kept me honest, as it were, by helping me stay close to the further education sector even though I have worked in universities for some years now: Crystalle Ahmed-Qureshi, and Clare Sutton.

Thanks to Routledge for taking this book on, especially to Sarah Hyde and Zoe Thomson, and to Faith Marsland for peerless copyediting.

Introduction

The term *Community of Practice* was first introduced in a slim book published in 1991 and then written about much more extensively in a further book published seven years later by one of the authors of the first one. Since then, the idea of **communities of practice** as places for learning, development, knowledge transfer, and so forth has travelled across many countries and been used to explore a sometime bewildering array of activities.

A small number of journal articles that used communities of practice (CoP) to talk about learning and teaching in further education colleges began to appear in the early 2000s, although it took much longer before they made their way into initial teacher education texts. They remain overshadowed within the initial teacher education curriculum by models derived from psychology, which were rarely reinforced through research done within the sector.

What I hope to do with this book is to change that, to provide a clear and compelling argument for looking at the work that further education colleges and adult education centres do from a CoP perspective. In order to do this, we need to take several steps.

First, we need to think about what CoPs actually are. Lots of people will tell you that they are setting up or facilitating communities of practice, but without a firm grasp of the key aspects of the theory, it's hard to know for sure. Second, we need to look at what previous researchers have done with CoP theory *in researching further and adult education*. Research from schools or universities simply will not do. There is not so much research about further and adult education from a CoP perspective as is the case with universities, for example, and what there is, is of variable quality. We need to be discerning, but we can nonetheless draw some robust conclusions. Third, we need to find a different way to talk about learning. CoP theory rests on learning – indeed, if you ever read something about CoPs that does not also talk about learning, without giving a good reason for not doing so, then you should put it down. CoP theory rests on a very specific model of learning that needs to be carefully described. Fourth, we need to think about how we might build a CoP from the ground up. This is not quite as straightforward as some might think, and requires the establishment of a **learning architecture**. Fifth, we need to evaluate CoPs. I do not mean evaluate in the manner of an inspection, however, but in terms of the claims that are made for them. What can they do? What can't they do? Sixth, we need to explore the different ways in which CoPs work alongside – or sometimes against – other CoPs. No CoP exists in isolation – they are all connected in different ways. Some are closely tied to others, and some are only very loosely linked. Seventh, we need to understand how assessment – the most characteristic activity of any formal educational institution – can be made sense of within a community of practice. And finally, we need to answer the most important question that pertains to *any* research or research-informed project: so what?

The eight chapters in this book have been arranged in a particular sequence, but I have provided some markers to allow for navigation around the text as a whole where necessary. The ideas that made up CoP theory are not entirely suitable for laying out in a line, and so I have done some judicious signposting to help the links across the chapters become clear. There is some academic jargon, but not too much, and I am not apologetic – lots of things have a specialist jargon attached to them. Key terms from CoP theory are in **bold** and other key theories from the literature are in *italics*, and I have provided a few references for further reading for those who wish to travel onwards. If more signposts or maps through the CoP terrain are needed, then please feel free to send me an email or a tweet.

1 What is a community of practice, and why do I need to know?

Introduction

In this first chapter, I am going to outline some of the key features of a Community of Practice. This won't be an exhaustive definition but it will be enough to get us started and to allow us to start to think about how the Community of Practice (CoP) approach can be used to think about the further education and skills sector. I will introduce a small number of key concepts and terms, and provide some links to real-world examples and previously published research that help to build our understanding of what CoPs are and how and where we might go looking for them within further and adult education. I am going to finish by providing one answer to the 'why do I need to know' question posed in the chapter title. During this chapter I will also introduce a few themes that will not be fully discussed until later in the book: you can read ahead if you like, but my advice is that you read Chapter 2 as well before starting doing so.

Getting to know Communities of Practice

Communities of Practice are everywhere. If you want to go looking for them, and you know what to look for, then you can find them in the places where people work, the places where people engage in pastimes and hobbies, and the places where people study. Researchers and academics have been writing about Communities of Practice for over three decades now, and they have written about a wide variety of them: adult learners in a basic skills class; architects; trainee nurses on placement; tailors; hairdressing apprentices; and trainee teachers in a further education college. These are all examples of Communities of Practice, and even though they are remarkable for their diversity, there are particular things happening within these distinct groups that means that we can describe each one as being a Community of Practice (CoP). Put simply, it is possible to consider a list of characteristics or qualities that each one of these groups can tick off, item by item. There are many different ways of describing groups of people when they join together to achieve, build, talk about, or share something. A CoP is just one of these – and it is a descriptor that, if used thoughtfully and carefully, can generate helpful and practical insights into whatever it is that the CoP is doing.

DOI: 10.4324/9781003252566-1

Working out whether a bunch of people all gathered together and doing something does in fact constitute a CoP is not hard. By this I mean to stress that there isn't a knotty tangle of concepts, jargon, or theories that make talking, writing and thinking about CoPs needlessly inaccessible. There are a few key terms and key concepts with their own specialist terminology, to be sure, but these are no more complicated or difficult to acquire than the specialist terminology that we might overhear in a car mechanics' workshop ('the steering has gone heavy'), trainee hairdressing salon ('we're going to be working with blocks today'), or NVQ assessors' staff room ('what are the level-2 range statements, please?') This is because one of the characteristics of any CoP is a specialist way of talking and perhaps writing as well (if writing is needed), in just the same way that a CoP might need specialist equipment or resources. These things – the talking and the equipment – are two parts of a bigger whole that in CoP theory is referred to as the **shared repertoire** of the CoP, and we will discuss shared repertoires later on in this chapter. For now, we will focus on what CoPs are, before turning to their characteristics or ingredients.

A Community of Practice is any group of people who share a focus, interest, goal, or body of work, and who are working together in order to learn about, practice, and then get done whatever it is that they are wanting to do. They are everywhere, and we are all members of lots of different ones. Some of them are mostly standalone, more-or-less isolated CoPs, whereas others will share things, routines, tools, methods, and even people. Sometimes we actively seek out membership, whereas at other times we might not even be aware that we are members. As people in the world, we engage in all kinds of activities or **practices** as part of our everyday lives: at work, at play, with families and/or with friends, with people who we hardly know, and with people who we share spaces with on a temporary basis. In order to take part in these practices people come together in **communities** so that they can talk to each other, share tools and materials, and, most importantly, learn more about what is being done and why. The people are usually pretty easy to identify, and it is often straightforward to work out who might be a member of a particular community, perhaps on account of the clothes that they wear, the tools or objects that they use, or the words and phrases that they employ in their writing or their speech.

This idea of the Community of Practice was first written about in a book published in 1991 called *Situated Learning: legitimate peripheral participation*, written by Jean Lave and Etienne Wenger. Jean Lave, who has now retired, was a professor at the University of California, and Etienne Wenger, who now works as an independent researcher and consultant, was one of her students and had completed his doctorate a year earlier. Lave and Wenger were part of a wider group of writers and researchers based at a number of universities who were interested in thinking about learning as an everyday activity and who did their research in 'real-life' settings ranging from hospitals to blacksmiths' workshops as well as classrooms, in contrast to the 'artificial' research conducted in laboratory settings by educational psychologists. Lave and Wenger's work rested on *anthropology* – the study of human societies and cultures. Lave and

Wenger's examples included tailors, midwives, and butchers (1991). Seven years later, Wenger published his book *Communities of Practice: learning, meaning and identity*. The examples of CoPs that were discussed in this later book included amateur radio operators, recovering alcoholics, and office-based computer users (1998). In the original book, they are only briefly discussed: the main focus of Lave and Wenger's earlier work is not the Community of Practice, but the discussion of a theory of learning (and we shall return to this in the following chapter). At that time, Lave and Wenger defined a Community of Practice as being 'largely an intuitive notion, which serves a purpose here but which requires a more rigorous treatment' (1991: 42). It fell to Wenger in his later book, and drawing on subsequent research, to provide that more rigorous treatment, through constructing a painstaking account of what CoPs are, how they work, and what they do. Subsequently, other researchers and writers have taken up the CoP as a way of thinking and writing about learning in a wide range of settings: art and design (Shreeve, 2007), mathematics (Solomon, 2007), tourism (Albrecht, 2012), aviation (O'Brien and Bates, 2015), literacy tutors (Sligo et al., 2019), and the UK fire and rescue service (Brooks et al., 2020). And there are many others. For example, I think that a further education college consists of a whole collection of CoPs (this is referred to by Wenger [1998] as a constellation – and we shall return to this in detail in Chapter 6), and I am going to draw on research as well as theory to make this argument as this book proceeds.

Perhaps unsurprisingly, the idea of what makes up a Community of Practice has changed over time. Wenger himself adopted a more practical and 'hands-on' approach in a subsequent book, *Cultivating Communities of Practice* (Wenger et al., 2002). In more recent work he has focussed more on the nature of professional knowledge across sets of multiple communities that he and his co-authors have described as a 'landscape' of practice (Wenger-Trayner et al., 2015), and on broader or looser groups that are called 'social learning spaces' (Wenger-Trayner and Wenger-Trayner, 2020). Meanwhile, other researchers and writers have drawn on their own research and theoretical insights in order to generate 'plug-ins' or 'updates' for CoP theory, for example in helping us to think about language within CoPs (Rock, 2005), or the ways in which CoPs might be found in online/digital spaces (Donnelly, 2008). Nonetheless, a core series of ideas about what a CoP is and how it works has persisted, based on the concepts established by Lave and Wenger (1991) and further discussed by Wenger (1998), and it is this group of ideas that forms the basis of the arguments that I am making here. Before we go any further, we need to establish the benchmarks of any CoP, and to open up our first discussion about CoP theory. But first I need to discuss very briefly why it is important to do so. Why should it matter whether or not this theory gets used 'properly' or 'rigorously'? Who am I to say that some of the things described as CoPs are just that, whilst others quite clearly are not, and yet more might in fact be CoPs but we cannot really be sure because they have not been discussed or researched with sufficient care and attention?

Interlude: reflecting on theory use and teacher education

After eight years working as an adult education tutor, I spent several years running teacher education programmes in FE colleges – Cert Ed and PGCE, and City and Guilds as well – before taking up my first post at a university. During my time working in FE colleges, and on many occasions since when I have visited colleges to give talks and run workshops, I have had conversations about the use and purpose of theory, sometimes in opposition to a more practical or hands-on approach to teacher education. What's the point in learning about these different theories? How do they actually help me teach my students? Broadly speaking, I am sympathetic to these sort of comments, not least as many teacher education curricula (and textbooks) for FE colleges and adult education contain theories that are either not based on research done in the sector, or are badly discussed and then applied, or have long since been discarded by academic writers but still live on as zombie theories in curriculum documents and textbooks, staggering about and refusing to die. Oftentimes, it's a combination of all three. So why should anybody pay attention to my argument that a CoP approach is worthwhile for teachers and trainers in further and adult education, whilst at the same time being told (by me – but by others as well) that learning-styles theories are a waste of time, that Maslow's Hierarchy of Needs is also not worth the effort, or that the concept of andragogy is best consigned to the rubbish bin?

The answer to all of this is in fact quite straightforward, which makes the persistence of these zombie theories in teacher education all the more regrettable. One of the things that a theoretical framework does is provide an explanatory framework – but it can only do this if it is also based on a solid body of research. Now, we can be generous in terms of how we define what good research looks like, but it is not the case that 'anything goes'. Educational research can be done in lots of ways (conducting extensive observations, large-scale surveys, interview-based studies, and so on) so long as it is done well, and carefully, within the approach that has been chosen. The research that underpinned learning styles has been thoroughly refuted (Coffield et al., 2004). As such it is not appropriate to suggest that 'even though the research is critical, learning styles might nevertheless be a helpful way to think about the differences between our learners': the theories are mistaken and misleading and have potentially harmful consequences and should therefore be rejected without hesitation. The research behind Maslow's Hierarchy of Needs has also been critiqued (Curzon and Tummons, 2013; Illeris, 2007) and the concept of andragogy in opposition to pedagogy has likewise long been debunked (Davenport, 1993). But again, both of these were based on insubstantial research and incoherent theorisation in the first place. The literature on Communities of Practice, by contrast, draws on substantial bodies of empirical research. Over time, different people have built on earlier CoP work and accumulate more robust theoretical understandings, as part of a much larger body of research and writing about learning and apprenticeship (some of this literature will be discussed in the following chapter). Yes, it can be the subject of critique, but not on the basis of being derived from insubstantial research or inadequate theorising. Instead, the critique comes from the standpoint of different academic disciplines such as cognitive psychology that occupy a fundamentally different worldview to the academic disciplines (anthropology and sociology) that have informed the development and evolution of CoP theories.

However, if CoP theories are going to remain robust and respected – even if not always agreed with – then it is important that rigorous research and theory work is continued. Simply put, without clear grounding in research or thorough use of the different elements of the theory, then we cannot tell whether or not something that is claimed to be a Community of Practice really is one, and we therefore lose the power for explanation and insight that a good theory can provide, as I shall discuss at different points throughout this book, and especially in Chapter 8.

Back to Communities of Practice: what are the three necessary ingredients of a CoP?

The first step in benchmarking a CoP, therefore, (and our first step in getting to know the specialist jargon of CoPs) is to look for these three ingredients: **mutual engagement, joint enterprise**, and **shared repertoire** (Wenger, 1998: 73–85). If you can make out all three of these in whatever social gathering – college, workplace, community centre, even online – you are interested in, then you are on the way to providing a rich and worthwhile, as well as useful, description of a Community of Practice (Tummons, 2018).

Mutual engagement

In order to get the work done (I am using the word 'work' generously here, to indicate anything that requires effort and application – it need not refer solely to employment) within a Community of Practice, the members of that community need to have systems, methods, processes, and so forth in place that will provide opportunities to talk, to share ideas, to swap notes, help each other out with tools or procedures, and so on. Different members of the CoP will go about this in different ways: some might prefer face-to-face meetings whereas others might prefer email. So long as the CoP has both methods set up, then it won't be a problem. Likewise, not all people will want and/or need more frequent opportunities for conversation, or for reading materials that are relevant to the work of the CoP. All of the ways through which the CoP members interact with each other in the doing of whatever they do is described by Wenger as **mutual engagement**. Some people are longstanding experts, and others are newbies. Some people pick up new techniques or ways of knowing quite quickly whilst others will need more time to practice. Working together isn't always harmonious, and people will sometimes disagree, want to do things a bit differently, perhaps even try something new – nothing stays the same, after all, and change can be found within all CoPs. Mutual engagement might always be done on a face-to-face basis or it might involve talking on the telephone as well as face to face, or meeting on Zoom or MS Teams, or posting messages on Facebook or Twitter. CoP members do not have to agree with each other all the time: things can be adjusted, argued over, tried differently, and spoken or even argued about in various ways so long as, in the end, everything that is being done/written/said/made, all links to the **joint enterprise** of the CoP.

Joint enterprise

Any CoP is always 'about' something. Sometimes, whatever it is that is the focus of the work done within the CoP – the mental, physical, or emotional effort that is required to keep the CoP going – can be quite tidily and easily defined; at other times, it might take a bit more work to say exactly what it is that the CoP does or is interested and engaged in – some will have explicit written rules and regulations, and others may rely on word of mouth, for example. But whether or not we are interested in a group of beauty therapists who all work full-time in the same salon, a group of model railway enthusiasts who pay a subscription to join a club that meets every Tuesday evening in a church hall, or a group of further education college assessors who meet on an online forum in order to discuss the moderation of portfolio-based assessments, these and all other CoPs will have a focus, a topic, a thing that they do. This is referred to as the **joint enterprise** of the community, but it is important to remember that the enterprise of the community does not have to always be agreed upon – it is in the doing of the work rather than the work itself that sufficient agreement needs to be found, or **negotiated**, in such a way that the CoP can keep working. The members of the CoP will always work out amongst and for themselves what is important and what is not, what needs to be done and what can be left behind, what is working well and what needs improving, and so forth. The joint enterprise of the community can stretch and relax over time, according to both internal and external pressures.

Shared repertoire

The third piece of the puzzle (for now) requires us to think about how the mutual engagement and the joint enterprise get done. For example: we know that one of the ways in which a CoP agrees on what it is going to be doing (joint enterprise) is through the members of the community talking to each other (mutual engagement). But how will they do this talking? By 'how' I don't mean to ask whether or not they will be meeting up in real life or deciding to use Zoom or even simply choose to do everything by email – that is the 'way' or 'method' of talking, not the 'how'. Instead, I mean to draw attention to how people in the CoP talk with, or write to, other members of the same CoP through using the particular words, phrases, and/or jargon that are specific to that CoP. Any community will always have a specific way of doing things – including talking – that helps speed the work along, and specialised ways of talking are just as useful within the CoP as specialised tools or methods are. Moreover, as we shall see in Chapter 2, it is in the picking up of how to talk or how to use the materials and equipment of a CoP that the practice of **learning** becomes visible. All of these elements – the ways of talking, the machinery, the routines, the tools and artefacts, the folders, the PDF files, the portfolios, and so on – are all gathered together as the **shared repertoire** of any given Community of Practice. Sometimes we can share these with other CoPs (this will be discussed in Chapter 6), and sometimes they are unique to just one CoP, perhaps even jealously guarded. But irrespective of whether or not they are commonplace or rare, highly technical or relatively commonplace, any and all aspects of the shared repertoire of the CoP need to be made available to any and all of the CoP members who might legitimately need to make use of them.

Mutual engagement, joint enterprise, and shared repertoire are three of the cornerstones of a CoP, therefore. There are other components to look for that all CoPs will possess in different ways, such as **boundaries** (which are pretty self-explanatory but do need some explanation – this will be covered in depth in Chapter 6), **trajectories** (which is how the journeys of the individual members within a CoP are described – this will be explored in Chapter 2), and **learning architectures** (which is a framework for building an environment for a new CoP – this will be discussed in Chapter 4). But these three – mutual engagement, joint enterprise, shared repertoire – provide enough detail to allow us to be sure that when we describe something as a CoP, it really is one. And in turn, we can now begin to think about the CoPs that we might find in a further education college, even across the sector as a whole, with a satisfactory degree of rigour and accuracy – a first step in careful and meaningful use of theory.

Looking for Communities of Practice

A lot of the time when I come across CoP stuff in relation to further education colleges or further education professionals, it is framed in terms of building or establishing a CoP. For example, the Education and Training Foundation (ETF) have in the past designed elements of their Advanced Practitioner development programme in terms of a 'Community of Practice element' (https://www.et-foundation.co.uk/news/2020-21-advanced-practitioner-programme-communities-of-practice-applications-open/). The Association for Learning Technology (ALT) carried out a 'Communities of Practice project' in 2020 to establish a successful 'community of practice' (CoP) where 'vocational teaching staff are able to acquire, develop and share the digital, and digital pedagogical, skills they need to thrive in vocational education' (https://www.alt.ac.uk/node/1257). Initiatives such as these are entirely praiseworthy and reflect the emergence of a revitalised professionalism in recent years. It is vital for teachers and trainers in further education and skills to have meaningful opportunities for professional development, for expanding and enriching their professional knowledge and competence, and for collaboration with colleagues in other parts of the country or other parts of the sector.

So what's the problem? Well, the problem is that it is difficult to ascertain whether or not what the ETF is doing is *actually* generating opportunities for CoPs to emerge, or whether something else is going to happen. Likewise, it is difficult to establish the extent to which all of the different organisations or groups of people that the ALT identified as CoPs in their report (https://www. alt.ac.uk/sites/alt.ac.uk/files/assets_editor_uploads/documents/ALT_Ufi%20Pro ject_CommunityAudit_Report_July%202020_2_public.pdf) really *are* CoPs, not least as the definition used in the report is very brief (https://www.learning-the ories.com/communities-of-practice-lave-and-wenger.html). Simply put, these are both examples of the kind of insufficient theory use that makes the whole thing a bit problematic. Simply saying that something is a CoP doesn't auto- matically mean that it is: you need to do your homework and establish, with some rich detail and careful description, *why* what you have got in front of you is a CoP. Only that way can we then go on to make use of the CoP theory in order to draw some useful conclusions and generate some meaningful insights. If a job is worth doing, then it is worth doing properly. Our next step, therefore, is to go looking for Communities of Practice, now that we know enough about what they look like and what they do to get us started, and we are sensitive to the need to be thorough and detailed in our descriptions of them. We shall save our discussions about building new CoPs for later in this book.

How to start? I want to put forward two ways to proceed: the first is through reading (this book, other books, other articles, and so forth) and per- haps talking with colleagues or friends who are also doing some of the same reading; the second is through research (as part of a PGCE/CertEd module or, more realistically, an Masters in Education project – I did my first CoP research as part of my end-of-module project during my MEd degree with the Open University) – which would require background reading in any case. It isn't compulsory to do your own research in order to bring CoP theory into your professional practice, but some careful reading and thinking is unavoidable (even if it's just this book!). I would always encourage teachers and trainers in the sector to think about doing a Masters degree, and it doesn't matter if you come from an academic or vocational background – initial teacher-training programmes are often a good route into the study of education more broadly. But whether or not we want to do a degree or simply do some reading, there always needs to be a sound rationale for our interests and inquiries. Thinking back to the earlier conversation about theory use, we need to answer one further question before getting started: why do we need to know about CoPs?

Communities of Practice: why do we need to know?

Thinking about shared repertoires, joint enterprises, trajectories, and so forth in purely abstract terms is of interest to some researchers and some theorists, of course, but the test of any good theory, arguably, is what it helps us do in the 'real world'. How does knowing about mutual engagement, boundaries, or learning architectures help tutors running plumbing and gas courses or delivering English as an Additional Language (EAL) programmes? In a way, the answer to this question is simple. My argument is that knowing about and therefore using CoP theory makes us better teachers, trainers, assessors, and colleagues. It enhances our professional knowledge and therefore our professionalism. It has benefits for us as individuals, for the colleges or adult education centres within which we work, and for the sector as a whole. It is not a quick fix, an easy way to encourage inclusive practice, or a method of guaranteeing collaboration or quality improvement (whatever those might mean). It's a shift in perspective, a framework for seeing and thinking about the work that we do in a slightly different way. CoP theory opens us up to thinking about the ways in which our teaching, training, and assessment practices can be more authentic and more meaningful for our students, apprentices, and trainees. And it also helps us think about our own work as *dual professionals* who work across two overlapping areas of expertise – that of being an educator, and that of being a subject specialist (Tummons and Ingleby, 2014).

As we travel through the subsequent chapters of this book, we will explore a number of different aspects of being a teacher/trainer in the FE sector. Some of them will be familiar to everyone and will be an important element of all of our professional lives, such as assessment and feedback, whilst other will be of relevance to only some areas of provision or curriculum, such as industrial placements. Employment and contractual responsibilities vary as well. Some of us will have programme or module leadership responsibilities (as I did when working in FE), whereas others will only have responsibility for teaching and for marking assignments (as was the case for me when I worked in adult education). Factors such as these all make a difference to our places – our **trajectories** – and thus to the nature of our work and learning – our **participation** – within the different CoPs that we are members of. Whether we are **full** or **peripheral** members of a CoP, we can still reflect on and theorise aspects of our work in the broadest sense – our pedagogic practice, our professional learning, the ways we give feedback, the ways we design our materials and resources – through the CoP lens. But so far, our discussions have been quite abstract, so perhaps it's time to turn to some concrete examples?

First example: the shared repertoire of tools and artefacts

As trainers or assessors, it is common practice for us to have to get to grips with course documentation containing information about *centre requirements* covering things such as candidate registration and certification, data protection, internal and external moderation, and so forth, or *learning outcomes* and *assessment criteria* that will list the skills, competencies, and so forth that each individual learner will be able to do upon successful completion of each individual unit that makes up the programme. Course documents such as these, which are a familiar part of our working lives as teachers, provide a good example of the **shared repertoire** of teachers and trainers in FE – whatever the subject specialism. Many of us have to read and write in them, help our trainees to complete their portfolios properly, get the portfolios from the entire cohort ready for internal verification, and so forth. They are a good example of **artefacts** that are found across a large number of CoPs in the further education and skills sector. If we drill down into a specific example of such an artefact, by contrast, then we can find our way into thinking about some tools and artefacts that are a little more specialised. For example, if we were to look at a typical set of course paperwork from City and Guilds such as the *Level 2 NVQ Diploma in Trowel Occupations* (https://www.cityandguilds. com/-/media/productdocuments/construction/construction/6570/6570_level_ 2/centre_documents/6570-04_l2_nvq_diploma_qualification_handbook.ashx), then we would quickly come across terms and phrases that relate to a more tightly bound subject specialism. For example: candidates will be required to learn how to install 'weep holes and vents' that allow for air and water circulation. Meanwhile, we might come across a very different meaning of the word 'vent' (this time, meaning a split in the back of a jacket for example to allow for ease of movement) when we read it in the scheme documentation for the City and Guilds *Level 3 Award / Certificate in Fashion.*

Second example: drawing up boundaries between different CoPs

It requires neither first-hand experience nor imagination to be confident that a CoP of brickwork is quite distinct from a CoP of fashion design. They might both be found within the same further education college and in fact there might even be some cross-border traffic between the two of them, but they are nonetheless different. The practice of brickwork is quite distinct from the practice of fashion design, and we can see the difference in watching what members of the two CoPs do as well as in how they use the same words – such as 'vent' – differently. We might not even need to be watching the members of a CoP at work in order to be able to work out which CoP they are members of: how people dress, for example, or whether people have to wear a badge on a lanyard, can indicate CoP membership. Even the jokes that people tell can give away details about the boundaries that divide CoPs – and the rivalries between them.

Several years ago when I was conducting my research into FE teacher education, I made several visits to a large land-based college to observe sessions and interview staff. One of the things that emerged during my visits was the rivalry between two of the curriculum areas, like a 'low-key' version of the rivalries that exist between supporters of different sports teams. The staff in the animal care and veterinary medicine programmes used to refer to the staff in the horticulture and agriculture department as the 'flower pickers'; in turn, the horticulture staff referred to the animal and veterinary staff as the 'bunny strokers'. In all other ways, it seemed to me after completing my visits, the staff all got along very well, and over time their mutual respect for each other did come through during our conversations.

It isn't really all that surprising to see that words have different meanings depending on the context within which they are used. But when we are within a Community of Practice, the specific meaning of a word takes on a particular kind of importance. The word – it might be 'vent' or it might be something else entirely – tells us something about the particular kind of work being done within the CoP in question. In turn, this leads us into thinking about other aspects of the **shared repertoire** of the CoP. What kind of tools or processes are involved in creating the vent? Do things need to be measured, or cut, or spaced? What kind of materials are involved? How big does a vent have to be? How many vents are needed? Thinking about the vent opens up the CoP to us, and comparing two different vents – one in a brick wall and one in the sleeve of a jacket – shows us how the same word works differently across two different CoPs, carrying different kinds of meanings, implying different kinds of activity, requiring different kinds of tools, and so forth. Likewise, one of the ways in which the members of a CoP support each other and nurture their community is through contrasting themselves with other groups. One of the central elements of any CoP is **identity** – both that of the CoP as a whole, but also of the individual members. Identity can be formed in several ways, partly as a consequence of learning through participating, but also through taking part in shared patterns of behaviour, including patterns of speech, use of particular jargon (as we saw in the first example, above) and even in shared jokes and histories, routines and habits.

These are both deliberately small-scale examples. At first look, you might think that focusing on 'vents' on the one hand and on 'flower pickers and bunny strokers' on the other is a bit trivial, and certainly not much help to us if we want to hold serious conversations about assessment or teaching resources, for example. But in fact, what these two examples are actually doing is providing 'entry points' into the two CoPs in question that do in fact hint at the more meaningful questions about learning and teaching that we are concerned with. The different use of the word 'vent' is just one example of any number of words or phrases that are used *in quite specific ways* within different CoPs, and if we, as teachers and trainers, are satisfied that our apprentices and students are using the words properly, then we can make legitimate assumptions about what has been learned and what has not, in just the same way that we can make inferences about the developing competence of our learners by watching how they hold and then manipulate a specific tool or piece of equipment. Crucially, these can be difficult for people who are *outside* the CoP to pick up on and recognise. This is not to say that the animal management staff don't have some sense of what it is that the horticulturalists do, and *vice versa*, but the fine-grained detail will almost certainly escape them.

Simply put, the people best positioned to make judgements about how the apprentices are doing are the longer-standing members of the CoP or, to use the expression given by Lave and Wenger (1991), the **old-timers**. And at the same time, mindful of the fact that within a CoP people are *always* learning (we will discuss this in Chapter 2), the people best positioned to make judgements about how the old-timers are doing are other old-timers in the same CoP. Old-timers from other CoPs within the **constellation** (the term used by Wenger to refer to linked networks of communities) might be able to help, however. Electrical installation tutors from one college would certainly be able to have meaningful conversations with electrical installation tutors at a different college. Their respective CoPs would have a great deal of overlap, allowing for ideas, people, routines, habits, and so forth to move between them fairly easily. Nonetheless we will have to remember that because they are different CoPs, some things will remain unique to each one. By contrast, someone from a more distant CoP would not be able to make such a helpful contribution. A catering and hospitality tutor (either from the same FE college as our electrical installers, or from a different college) would be able to say something about more generic issues such as the importance of keeping the learners' tracking documentation up-to-date, or the need to update the college virtual learning environment with materials for the apprentices' portfolios, but issues such as these are only a secondary rather than primary aspect of the practice of the community.

We are now in a position to provide a first answer to the 'why CoPs' question (there will of course be more answers to this question in later chapters of this book). Consider the common practice of observation of teaching and learning (OTL) within the sector. Observations are used to prepare for inspection, as part of internal quality-assurance processes, and as a form of staff development. But who is doing the observing? Even with high levels of observer training, proformas, handbooks and checklists, and published observation policies and guidelines, an outsider can *never fully understand* what goes on within a particular CoP. Even if they are from a closely related CoP, there will be things going on within the CoP being observed that they cannot fully appreciate or make sense of. The more distant the CoP from which the observer comes, the more distant the capacity for understanding. And this is our first insight through the CoP lens: observations by outsiders of any kind will always be restricted, perhaps even flawed to some degree. Certainly, the 'outsider-observer' will never be able to recognise fully all of the things that are happening within the CoP. And the implications of this for OTLs, as well as for other forms of evaluation and assessment, will be discussed in more depth in Chapter 7.

The insights that we might glean from CoP theories are not only about assessment and evaluation, however. A CoP perspective can give us new ways of thinking about learning and can help us answer questions such as 'how do we know when someone has learned something new?' or 'how do we know when someone has got good at something?' We can find new ways of thinking about the equipment, activities, and resources that we use with our trainees and apprentices, not only in terms of how they can interest and engage our students, but in terms of how they relate to the topics or subjects – the **practice** – that they, and we as tutors and lecturers, are a part of. A CoP standpoint can help us think about students' transitions into FE colleges after leaving school or after deciding on a career change later in life, how students make sense of the different courses or modules that they are working towards, and where they might go after completing their programmes of study and learning. The same CoP lens can help us as teachers and trainers to look at feedback differently, rethink the place of functional skills within different areas of the curriculum, and enhance the importance of our subject specialisms. It can help us appreciate all of the things that FE colleges and adult education providers do well that, for various reasons, do not always get recognised. And it can give us, as practitioners, a way of thinking and speaking about our work, our **practice**, that demands both attention and respect.

Some conclusions

In this first chapter we have discussed some of the key ingredients of any Community of Practice – the mutual engagement, joint enterprise, and shared repertoire – that can help us identify a CoP at work. We have also introduced several of the other important elements of CoP theory – trajectories, full and peripheral membership, learning architectures, and boundaries – which will be discussed in more depth in later chapters. We have considered the importance of using CoP theory properly in order to generate meaningful and worthwhile ideas and insights and we have briefly considered some 'bad theories' or 'zombie theories' that are best avoided. I am not suggesting that this theory is the answer to everything, and nor would any other self-respecting academic. In Chapter 5, the strengths as well as the limitations and restrictions of CoPs will be discussed in a critical manner. Nonetheless, we can already see how a CoP perspective might not only inform our professional practice but also challenge aspects of our professional working lives.

References

Albrecht, J. (2012) Authentic Learning and Communities of Practice in Tourism Higher Education. *Journal of Teaching in Travel and Tourism* 12 (3) 260–276. doi:10.1080/15313220.2012.704254.

Brooks, J., Grugulis, I., and Cook, H. (2020) Rethinking situated learning: participation and communities in the UK fire and rescue service. *Work, Employment and Society* 34 (6) 1045–1061. doi:10.1177/0950017020913225.

Coffield, F., Moseley, D., Hall, E., and Ecclestone, K. (2004) *Should We Be Using Learning Styles? What research has to say to practice.* London: Learning and Skills Research Centre.

Curzon, L.B. and Tummons, J. (2013) *Teaching in Further Education: an outline of principles and practice.* Seventh edition. London: Bloomsbury.

Davenport, J. (1993) Is there any way out of the andragogy morass? In Thorpe, M., Edwards, R. and Hanson, A. (eds.) *Culture and Processes of Adult Learning.* London: Routledge/Open University. 109–117.

Donnelly, R. (2008) Virtual Problem-based Learning Communities of Practice for Teachers and Teacher Educators: An Irish Higher Education Perspective. In Kimble, C. and Hildreth, P. (eds.) *Communities of Practice: Creating Learning Environments for Educators.* Vol. 2. Charlotte, NC: Information Age Publishing. 67–88.

Illeris, K. (2007) *How We Learn: learning and non-learning in school and beyond.* London: Routledge.

Lave, J. and Wenger, E. (1991) *Situated Learning: Legitimate Peripheral Participation.* Cambridge: Cambridge University Press.

O'Brien, W. and Bates, P. (2015) Looking and feeling the part: developing aviation students' professional identity through a community of practice. *Teaching in Higher Education* 20 (8) 821–832. doi:10.1080/13562517.2015.1087998.

Rock, F. (2005) 'I've picked some up from a colleague': language, sharing and communities of practice in an institutional setting. In Barton, D. and Tusting, K. (eds.) *Beyond Communities of Practice: Language, Power and Social Context*. Cambridge: Cambridge University Press. 77–104.

Shreeve, A. (2007) Learning development and study support: an embedded approach through communities of practice. *Art, Design and Communication in Higher Education* 6 (1) 11–25. doi:10.1386/adch.6.1.11_1.

Sligo, F., Tilley, E., Murray, N., and Comrie, M. (2019) Community of practice versus community of readers: the literacy tutors' dilemma. *Journal of Vocational Education and Training* 71 (1) 108–125. doi:10.1080/13636820.2018.1464052.

Solomon, Y. (2007) Not belonging? What makes a functional learner identity in undergraduate mathematics? *Studies in Higher Education* 32 (1) 79–96. doi:10.1080/03075070601099473.

Tummons, J. (2018) *Learning architectures in higher education: beyond communities of practice*. London: Bloomsbury.

Tummons, J. and Ingleby, E. (2014). *The A to Z of Lifelong Learning*. Maidenhead: McGraw Hill.

Wenger, E. (1998) *Communities of Practice: Learning, Meaning and Identity*. Cambridge: Cambridge University Press.

Wenger, E., McDermott, R. and Snyder, W. (2002) *Cultivating Communities of Practice*. Boston, MA: Harvard Business School Press.

Wenger-Trayner, E., Fenton-O'Creevy, M., Hutchinson, S., Kubiak, C. and Wenger-Trayner, B. (eds) (2015) *Learning in Landscapes of Practice: boundaries, identity and knowledgeability in practice-based learning*. London: Routledge.

Wenger-Trayner, E. and Wenger-Trayner, B. (2020) *Learning to make a difference: value creation in social learning spaces*. Cambridge: Cambridge University Press.

2 Where is the learning in a Community of Practice, and how does it happen?

Introduction

In this second chapter, we shall turn our attention to learning and specifically to the theory of learning that lies at the heart of CoP theory. All too often, people using CoP theory do not pay much attention to the learning that is taking place, and often do not go into much detail about what is being learned, or how. This has the effect of weakening the use of the theory overall. The theory of learning that CoPs rest on is one of several theories of learning as social practice, and these have emerged after decades of research and writing in opposition to the ideas derived from psychology that are often found in teacher education curricula. In this chapter, two additional key elements of CoP theory will be introduced alongside the theory of learning: the concept of learner trajectories, and the concept of change within communities of practice. With the hairdressing curriculum providing a worked example, we shall frame these ideas within recognisable, authentic contexts. In this chapter, I deliberately slide between the ideas to be found in Lave and Wenger (1991), which relate more closely to the learning of apprentices or newcomers, and ideas to be found in Wenger (1998), which provide a more extensive social theory of learning.

Different ways of thinking about learning

A few days ago (at the time of writing) I was visiting a further education college where the programme leader for the PGCE/CertEd pathway talked me through some of the changes that they were making to their curriculum in response to a recent Ofsted inspection. The college had been going through a restructure and the initial teacher education (ITE) department had not been well-served by this. At the time of the inspection, the previous programme leader had been off sick and the teaching was being done entirely by hourly paid staff – all good people but not in a position to lead the college through the inspection process. One of the changes being made in response to the Ofsted inspection, and drawing on the college leaders' reading of Ofsted documentation, was to push two particular approaches to learning and teaching to the forefront of the ITE curriculum. The first of these was *Rosenshine's Principles of Instruction*, and the second was *Cognitive*

DOI: 10.4324/9781003252566-2

Science – both very much in favour with Ofsted. Rosenshine's principles – there are ten of them in the original pamphlet from 2010 – do not make up a theory of learning but instead are a list of ten things that make for good and effective teaching, all based on Rosenshine's own analysis of a range of different research articles and books that in several cases rested on cognitive science. Cognitive science is the study of mind and intelligence, and rests predominantly on psychology. As I write this, the cognitive science approach to thinking about teaching and learning is enjoying a great deal of influence: the government likes it, Ofsted likes it, and organisations such as ResearchED promote it through their workshops and publications. Thanks to this political support, it is not surprising to see it starting to appear in the FE sector, even though hardly any of the cognitive science research has been done in colleges or adult education centres.

Cognitive science is just one of a number of different schools of thought that have emerged over time in relation to learning, and therefore to teaching as well. Other branches of psychology such as behaviourism and neo-behaviourism are also commonly found in teacher-training textbooks, and humanistic psychology has been more influential in adult education specifically, but overall these have waned in popularity recently in comparison to cognitive science. What they all have in common, however, is a focus on the individual learner. Behaviourism and neo-behaviourism are both concerned with the study and control of observable behaviour on the part of the student, humanist psychology foregrounds the importance of the student's self-fulfilment, and cognitive science focuses on memory and mental processes. These are of course all very brief summaries – but I do not want to spend a lot of time talking about these groups of theories because extensive descriptions are easy to find elsewhere. What I want to do instead is to consider this question: what if these psychological models are all thinking about things the wrong way around, focussing on the individual's behaviour, short- or long-term memory or cognitive processes, when we should be focussing our attention on the contexts – the places – where learning is happening and on people as a whole instead of just cognition? What if these psychological models are not as robust or as comprehensive in providing answers as they might first appear?

Thinking differently about what learning might be: from psychology to social practice

Before Jean Lave and Etienne Wenger wrote their book *Situated Learning*, Lave spent many years doing research into how and what people learned outside formal educational settings. She spent several years during the 1970s researching apprentice tailors in Liberia (Lave and Wenger, 1991: 69–73) and later focussed on how people used mathematics in everyday life through the *Adult Math Project* – AMP (Lave, 1988). For the AMP, 35 people – mostly female – were observed over time as they did their supermarket shopping, put their groceries away and planned their meals, organised their household food budgets, and so forth – taking about 40 hours per person (that's 1400 hours just for the data collection, never mind the analysis and writing up – this was a substantial research project!). The idea behind the project was to look at the ways that people used different kinds of arithmetic or mathematics in their everyday lives. At the time of the AMP study – the late 1970s and early 1980s – supermarkets rarely had computerised checkout systems and people did not have computers at home, so budgeting, financial planning and so forth – whether for food shopping or for other household bills – would be done using arithmetic. After collecting all of the research data, Lave then classified the *types* of arithmetic that people were using in their day-to-day lives, and then got them all to do school-style tests. In the tests, the AMP people were asked to do the same kinds of arithmetic that they had been observed doing in their everyday lives, but this time 'converted' into the kinds of abstract or generic problems that are familiar to all of us from school.

What Lave found was that when people were doing their school-style tests, they could no longer do the arithmetic that they had been observed doing perfectly well on multiple occasions when doing their shopping: they were successful in their 'everyday' maths but not in their 'school-style' maths. Amongst the conclusions that Lave drew from this research, two stand out as being particularly important for our present conversation about learning. First, she challenged the idea that successful learning – from the point of view of psychological models – would always involve being able to *transfer* what has been learned to a new context. That is to say, if you have learned something properly at school you would then be able to transfer what you have learned to a different setting – or *vice versa*. Second, she challenged the idea that the failure to transfer learning in this way is a result of a cognitive incapacity on the part of the individual. All of the people in the AMP study evidently did not have a cognitive incapacity even though they scored so badly on their 'school-style' tests, because they could do the arithmetic in 'real life'.

Alongside her prior research with apprentice tailors, Lave interpreted her findings from the AMP project as showing very clearly that learning needed to be understood as being not transferable or generalisable, but more specific, **situated** within different social settings or contexts. Nor was she alone in conducting this kind of research. Numerous other writers and researchers were, at the same time, challenging classical psychology, researching contexts as diverse as psychotherapy, naval navigation, mothers helping children to learn things in the home, blacksmiths, and schoolchildren with special educational needs (Chaiklin and Lave, 1996). This broader field of academic work helped to generate an alternative to a psychological perspective on learning – a *social practice* or *social theory* perspective on learning.

Interlude: what's 'wrong' with psychology?

Actually, it isn't really the case that psychology is 'wrong', but that it rests on a series of mistaken assumptions. Therefore the argument that I am outlining here is that the impact of psychology on what we think about teaching specifically and formal education more generally needs looking at. Following Lave (1988), we can identify four things about classical psychology that we are in turn going to challenge through using social practice theories more generally and Communities of Practice theory specifically (Curzon and Tummons, 2013).

1   The research done by psychologists and the conclusions that they draw are assumed to be straightforwardly transferable from laboratory settings to the outside world – to 'real life'.
2   Psychological theories have shaped not only educational theories but also educational practices. The psychologists' focus on cognition means that intellectual work is seen as being more important than practical work and, therefore, the academic curriculum is seen as being more important than the vocational or technical curriculum.
3   The academic curriculum rests on the idea that if people study a particular group of subjects, then this will form a mental discipline that will – in general – improve the minds of the students. This adds to the idea that those academic subjects are 'more important' or 'more worthwhile' than others.
4   Over time, a contrast has been drawn between 'scientific' knowledge and 'everyday' knowledge. The knowledge that is said to be contained within the academic curriculum is assumed to be more important than the 'everyday' knowledge found in working or family life.

Anybody who has worked in the further and adult education sectors will recognise some of these factors at work. The ways in which vocational and technical subjects are seen as being 'less important' than academic subjects, for example, will be very familiar to those of us who try to push back against labels such as 'the second chance sector' that FE has been described with in the past. Likewise, the idea of 'mental discipline' through studying particular subjects is used to further privilege the academic curriculum over the technical or vocational curriculum, with the latter dismissed as being 'easier' for people who are not 'clever' enough for academic subjects. But we all know that this isn't true: I have very clear memories – from my PGCE/CertEd days – of sitting in during electrical installation, nail technician, and web design classes: just three examples of curricula that are highly demanding in 'cognitive' as well as 'practical' ways. But when learning within a Community of Practice, the cognitive-practical divide doesn't exist (so we can throw out Bloom's taxonomy of learning – which, it is important to note, was not based on any serious empirical research): as we shall see, learning involves the whole person.

From social practice to Community of Practice: social models of learning

Communities of Practice theory is just one example of a family of social practice theories in just the same way that there are different schools of psychological theory. As you might expect, different theorists and writers have emphasised rather different things, but social practice theories of learning do all share some common ground. Instead of focusing entirely on the mind, on mental function and behaviour, social practice theories focus on the whole person – what a student or apprentice can do is as important as what they can remember. Accordingly, knowing something is not purely or solely a mental process, but a process that has an impact on the whole person – how they think, talk, act, use tools and materials, and interact with their environment. Social practice theories do not try to split up the academic and the vocational, or the cognitive and the practical: taxonomies such as cognitive/psycho-motor/affective domains of learning are rejected because these are seen as false, even misleading divisions. Similarly, social practice theories do not make a distinction between formal learning or informal learning – learning is 'the same' wherever it is taking place. It is never an individual process but always a shared one – a **social** one. It happens all of the time, even if we don't always realise it, and – most importantly – always happens as a consequence of **practice**. A social practice model of learning is about more than 'just' apprenticeship or learning by doing however. It also includes learning by talking and thinking, learning by writing, and learning by listening. Learning involves the whole person and the whole body. Put simply, people learn things from being able to take part in practice, to try things out. Being able to ask other more experienced people how things are done, which tool or procedure would be best used for a particular task and when and so forth is an important part of this practice. And in a college, those more experienced people are the trainers and teachers (the practice of teaching will be discussed in Chapter 4).

Communities of Practice theory rests on a particular version of social learning theory, explored in depth by Wenger (1998) but first introduced, as a particular way of discussing apprenticeship learning, in Lave and Wenger's original book (1991). In fact, as I noted in Chapter 1, the idea of the CoP was only briefly discussed in the first book, whereas their model of learning was more extensively explored. For Lave and Wenger, apprenticeship is the main focus for attention and their model has quite a cumbersome name – **legitimate peripheral participation** (LPP) – but it does in fact neatly sum up what the theory is all about and how it slots into the CoP model, and so it is worth our while to unpack LPP. An understanding of LPP is one of the central ideas to making sense of how CoPs work because entry to the CoP requires learning through Legitimate Peripheral Participation.

Exploring Legitimate Peripheral Participation

Before we go any further, we need to spend some time thinking about what Legitimate Peripheral Participation (LPP) actually is. There are two elements to this conversation: the first is to approach LPP as one element of a social theory of learning (Wenger, 1998), and the second is to weave LPP into a Community of Practice. Remember: learning is a necessary ingredient of any

Community of Practice, no matter how quickly or slowly (for example) that learning might be happening. As our discussion of LPP proceeds, we will introduce a small number of additional elements of CoP theory to add to those introduced in Chapter 1.

What is Legitimate Peripheral Participation? The most straightforward way to define it is to go backwards, and start with **participation**, which we have already introduced. Every member of a Community of Practice engages with – participates in – whatever it is that the CoP is about. Participation is a fundamental aspect of community **membership**, for newbies as well as old-timers, and it is not possible to be a member of a CoP without also participating in what the CoP does, even if that participation is only marginal, at a very basic or **peripheral** level. Because membership relies on participation in what the CoP is actually about, the participation has to be the 'real thing' – it has to be authentic or, to put it another way, it has to be **legitimate**.

Remembering one of the important messages from Chapter 1 – that CoPs are already out there in the world and that it is simply the case that we have to go looking for them – it is a straightforward exercise to imagine LPP at work. An easy example is to think about the work being done in a high street hair and beauty salon. All of the people who work there are members of that CoP, but in different ways or at different levels. The newcomers might be working and studying for NVQs at the same time, or they might have done a college course and then got a job – they are members in the same way that the senior stylists are members, but at first they are only allowed to do a specific, ring-fenced number of tasks such as shampooing customers' hair, sweeping and tidying up, even making drinks for the clients (Billett, 1998, 2007). From this perspective, the ways in which traditional ideas about apprenticeships were drawn on by Lave and Wenger (1991) can be easily seen. Over time, the apprentice or newcomer is given the opportunity to try new things, by observing and copying with the more experienced community member on hand: this might be something as straightforward as being shown how to use the appointment booking software, or something more complex such as hair colouring.

Hair colouring, as just one example of the **joint enterprise** of the hairdressing community, requires people to learn about all kinds of things ranging from using the International Colour Chart (ICC – a number-based system used throughout the industry to classify hair colour) to describe principles of colour selection, using and cleaning the correct equipment, actually mixing and applying the colour, and providing aftercare advice to the client. It involves both 'theoretical' and 'practical' knowledge and know-how, although as advocates of CoP theory we would reject this divide and say that all of the knowing is the same because it is all necessary in order to engage in practice – or, to put it another way, it is all necessary for **mutual engagement**. It involves learning about and using many tools and materials. Some of these will be familiar because they can be found in many other CoPs as well: examples include mixing bowls and measuring flasks, towels and cotton wool. Others, meanwhile, are very specific elements of the hairdressing CoP: climazone hair dryers, sectioning clips, emulsion lighteners.

Whether found only within hairdressing or also elsewhere, these materials – the physical objects, their names, how they are used – all nonetheless form part of the **shared repertoire** of this CoP. For the new member or apprentice learning about hair colouring (or indeed about anything else that is part of the shared repertoire), the techniques that they acquire ('pulled through' or 'weaved'), the specialist terminology ('full head' or 'regrowth application') that they use and the habits that they adopt ('communicate with the client in a professional manner'), are all elements of what is learned through LPP within the CoP. As time goes on, our hairdressing apprentice will be shown how to mix colours, how best to consult with the client, and how to apply the colour and post-colour treatment to the client's hair. The apprentice will become more fluent, more adept, at hair colouring – and also more fluent and adept in all of the other aspects of the hairdressing community that they need to get good at in order to move from being a **peripheral** member to being a **fuller** member.

Learning and membership – from being peripheral to being full

Both learning and membership are key features of any CoP, therefore, and they are each related to the other. Being a member of a CoP automatically means that our newcomer is doing some learning, even if they don't realise that it's happening. And the more authentic or legitimate learning they do, the fuller their membership becomes. They start at the side lines or periphery, and travel in a fuller direction as they learn, becoming more expert, more proficient, more knowledgeable and competent as they go. This direction of travel through/across a CoP is referred to as the learner's **trajectory** (Lave and Wenger, 1991: 18–19; Wenger, 1998: 153–6). As we might imagine, different members of a CoP might not necessarily share the same trajectories. What if our hairdressing apprentice decides that this is not the career for them after finishing their level two qualification and decides to try something different? What if one of the senior stylists at a salon, or the senior tutor at a training salon within a further education college, decides to change career, perhaps to work for an industry supplier, or for a professional or awarding body?

Trajectories such as these help us start to think about how members might travel from one CoP to another, so long as it is not too distant or different, or even how they can juggle being members of several overlapping communities at once. We shall think about **multimembership** in more depth in Chapter 6: for now, it is sufficient to remember that being a member of lots of CoPs is not uncommon, and that some of these CoPs will be closely linked or overlapping, whilst others might be quite distinct. Any CoP always contains members who are travelling across different trajectories, therefore. Lave and Wenger originally conceived of trajectories as being 'extremely diverse and [not] predictable' (1991: 19) but otherwise provided relatively little detail. Wenger (1998: 154–155) identified five specific kinds of trajectory, and as CoP research and theory has evolved, other writers have proposed additional elements to trajectories in turn that will be explored in later chapters of this book (Handley et al., 2006; Tummons, 2018).

Trajectories within and across Communities of Practice (Wenger, 1998)

- **Peripheral trajectories.** Peripheral trajectories are those trajectories that are never – by design – intended to lead to fuller participation. This might be due to the way in which a CoP has evolved over time, or this might be due to the individual member deciding that they do not want to aim for full participation.
- **Inbound trajectories.** Inbound trajectories are those trajectories that aim to allow full participation. The member will start at the periphery, but is committed/allowed/expected to continue working/learning in order to move to a fuller position, with a greater depth of participation, within the CoP.
- **Insider trajectories.** The idea of the insider trajectory helps us to think about what happens to a CoP member once they have reached a fuller state of membership. This is not to say that their membership is as full as it can be because – as we shall see – CoPs change over time so there is always more to learn. Instead fuller membership entails being able to contribute to the evolution of the practice of the community.
- **Boundary trajectories.** In contrast to insider or peripheral trajectories, boundary trajectories are those pathways followed by members who – for various reasons (we shall explore this in Chapter 6) – either prefer or are required to participate at the boundary of a CoP, perhaps crossing over to the boundary of another CoP as well.
- **Outbound trajectories.** Finally, there are those trajectories that lead out of a CoP, either through design because membership was only ever intended as being fixed-term, or through choice, because the individual member has decided to move on to something different – or been asked to do so by others within the CoP.

Thinking about participation in terms of these different trajectories allows us to make sense of the different kinds of journeys taken by people that are recognisable to anyone who has worked in an FE college or for a training provider. It doesn't matter if we are focussing on students/apprentices, or on tutors/old-timers. They are all CoP members and therefore are all learning as a consequence of their participation in practice. For the apprentices, learning is through **legitimate peripheral participation**, affording them entry into the community. For the old timers, **full participation** continues to generate opportunities for learning. The difference between apprentices and old-timers is in what, not how, they are learning, and this is a reflection of their different trajectories and/or places within any particular CoP. Sometimes, our trajectory within one CoP will directly relate to our trajectory within another one (this is another feature of CoP **multimembership**). Our participation and our learning within one CoP can make a difference to our participation and our learning in another.

Trajectories for learning in Communities of Hairdressing Practice

As with many other professions, there is more than one way to become a hairdresser. At the different colleges that I have visited (or worked with via Microsoft Teams because of covid) during the past few years, all bar one had a training salon on site that offered a range of courses across the broader hair and beauty curriculum. For some apprentices, studying at college and then going on to work in a salon provides the ideal route; others, however, may prefer to undertake a formal apprenticeship (intermediate and advanced options might be available), which will involve working in paid employment for four days a week and then attending college on the fifth. Or it might even be possible to gain full-time employment with the expectation that learning on the job will be accompanied by a college course in the employee's own time and at their own expense. We can easily picture, therefore, a collection or **constellation** of Communities of Hairdressing Practice. Some of these CoPs will be at individual salons, and some will be at individual FE colleges. Depending on the career progression routes chosen and on which routes are available, we might find that an individual learner is enrolled at a college-based CoP and does all of their **practice** at the training salon. Or we might find a learner employed – probably as an apprentice – in a salon on the high street, which is the setting for the bulk of their **practice**, with smaller amounts of time spent at the college as well: this would be an example of **multimembership**.

Let's start with the student enrolled on the college-based course, attending college every day, learning their profession in a training salon designed in such a way so as to replicate a 'real life' salon. Providing such authentic environments for *work-related programmes* is very common within FE colleges: some of the colleges that I have visited over the years have had hair and beauty salons, restaurants, bakeries, motor-vehicle workshops, and even a section of an aeroplane cabin for the cabin-crew training programme, and the maintenance of these environments is invariably part of course or centre approval by awarding bodies. But there are several significant differences between the training salon and the high street salon. The training salon is situated within an FE college – it is physically as well as culturally separate from the commercial environment of a high street. It is only seldom open to the public, is predominantly worked in by learners, and has only a relatively small number of professionally qualified staff. And there are other differences in practice as well: you would, for example, be very unlikely to walk into a high street salon and find all of the hairdressers practicing with blocks (model heads for training, with real hair) or working on embedded numeracy or literacy skills. What else might we need to know about our college student as they start their new course? They will almost certainly need to wear their college ID card on a lanyard around their neck or clipped to a pocket. They will probably have to be in uniform as well. At one of the colleges I worked at, the hairdressing students were in black college uniform, the beauty therapy students wore white, and the massage and holistic therapy students wore brown, making the three different CoPs within the hair and beauty department easy to identify.

It is not too difficult for us to find out what our new hairdressing trainee will be learning during their time at college, since awarding bodies publish their curriculum documents – materials for tutors as well as workbooks for candidates – online. Of more interest to our inquiry, however, is the **trajectory** that is 'mapped out' for the trainee. The trainee is the newcomer within the college-based Community of Hairdressing Practice and the lecturer is the old-timer, but the trainee probably does not enter this specific CoP with the intention of becoming a college-based lecturer: they are more likely to want to complete two years at college and then gain employment in the industry, at a salon. Or, to put it another way, the trainee is following a **peripheral trajectory**, not an **inbound trajectory**, within this particular CoP. The trainee's time within the CoP will only ever be limited to a particular group of the **practices** that are to be found within it, whilst other practices will always be restricted to the experts or old-timers – the tutors. The tutors are more expert hairdressers, of course, which is a necessary prerequisite for being able to teach hairdressing skills to the learners, but they also have some expert knowledge and experience that relates to their 'being a tutor' practice within the college generally and the CoP specifically. This is an example of the *dual professionalism* that characterises the FE teacher workforce – an aspect of the **joint enterprise** of the college-based CoP that belongs only to the tutors, who will be following **insider trajectories**. These trajectories entail learning about things such as how to plan a curriculum, how to deliver feedback, or how to organise internal moderation and external validation. These are all aspects of the **practice** of a college tutor (or adult education tutor – the days of non-accredited, recreational adult learning are sadly long gone) that in lots of ways are shared with tutors in other subject areas (and we shall discuss this in Chapter 6) but which are nonetheless specific to hairdressing. Curriculum planning requires an understanding of the subject specialism. Valid and reliable assessment (discussed in Chapter 7) likewise requires a thorough understanding of not only the subject specialism but also the assessment criteria, learning outcomes, and so forth.

As many of us who have worked in an FE college will know (and you don't have to have worked in one for a particularly long time), things often change and new things have to be learned as a consequence. For example: an awarding body might rewrite some of the units within a programme; the college might require the hairdressing team to move from City and Guilds to NCFE; or the teaching staff might need to update their hairdressing skills. As well as being further examples of things that we might find along an **insider trajectory**, they are also examples of how *everyone* within a CoP needs to always be learning, on this occasion as a result of the practices on the community themselves changing or evolving. The practices of hairdressing have changed over time due to new technologies and new techniques, as well as changes in style or taste, and these will all eventually find their way into the curriculum: as a result, tutors and trainers will need to stay up-to-date, to refresh and renew their professional hairdressing skills. To put it another way, the Communities of Hairdressing Practice have changed.

Interlude: changes in practice, changes in learning

No CoP stands still. Change is a characteristic of every Community of Practice, whether or not the pace of change is so slow as to be barely noticeable, or so fast that we can hardly keep up. Change can be gradual or incremental, or can come in fits and starts. It can be caused by inventions and improvisations, by happy accidents or in response to difficulties. Social practices of all kinds (hairdressing, hat-making, heavy metal music) do not stand still, and nor do the communities that provide social and cultural spaces for these practices to be engaged with. If practice changes, it follows that participation changes, and in turn that the things that must be learned will also change as well. For temporary members of a CoP who follow a **peripheral trajectory**, the changes may well not even be noticeable because their time spent within the CoP might not be long enough for the next round of changes to take effect. For those on **inbound** and **insider trajectories**, these changes will require some new learning.

An example of a change that is a live issue at the time of writing is the introduction of *T Levels*. As a new model for delivering the vocational and technical curriculum, T Levels will require tutors to learn some new procedures and systems – new **practices** – relating to all those ways in which T Levels are different to existing vocational qualifications in terms of delivery and so forth. Tutors will have to get acquainted with new systems for assessment and moderation, for example, and systems for work placements (which are a core component of any T-Level programme). This new 'T-Level learning' does not directly impact on the **joint enterprise** of our Community of Hairdressing Practice in relation to the doing, learning, or assessing of hairdressing, but it does impact on the practice of the CoP in relation to the work of learning and teaching that also forms part of what the community does. This does not affect the students (it seems unlikely that lots of people will swap from NVQs to T Levels) but it does affect the tutors, who will have to learn a number of new things relating to their professional role as educators. Nor will T Levels affect only hairdressing communities: many other CoPs across FE colleges, and the sector as a whole, will also have to shift and adapt aspects of what they do. More generic issues such as these are familiar to tutors and trainers across many subject specialisms – as such, as we shall see in Chapter 6, they can be found across **constellations** of CoPs and involve processes that often cross the **boundaries** between different communities.

If we think back to our hairdressing trainee arriving at college for the first time, we can now place them on a trajectory that is clearly different from the trajectory followed by their tutor: they are both learning, and learning relies on practice for both of them. But the trainee is clearly embarking on a journey to join and become a member of the CoP whilst the tutor is already in it. The trainee is more peripheral than the tutor, but they are both participating in practice. The ways that they both learn – through practice – and the nature of that learning – as a fundamental process that affects the entire person – is the same: that is what is meant by a social theory of learning.

Other trajectories and other communities

If we imagine a second trainee, this time employed in a salon and studying for an apprenticeship on a part-time basis, we might easily imagine that they would want to continue working at that same salon one day when fully qualified, either as an employee or on a self-employed basis, renting a chair. They might do all of their training whilst working at one salon (a level 2 apprenticeship would normally take two years, so they might be ready for a change) and then leave to work, and perhaps to continue studying for a level 3 apprenticeship at a different one, whereas our first trainee will work at a salon only after finishing their college course. Different trajectories within different CoPs, but with several things in common – as is the case with any **constellation** of communities.

What is most important for our analysis at this moment is a comparison of the **trajectories** that both of our trainees are following. Our trainee at the salon might easily imagine working at that same salon one day – moving on a trajectory that is increasingly full. It is far less likely that our college-based trainee imagines working at the college in the future (although it could happen, it is an unlikely outcome). Our salon trainee is following a trajectory that is aligned to those ideas relating to directions of travel within CoPs, with newcomers at the edges – the periphery – imagining fuller participation in the future (Lave and Wenger, 1991; Wenger, 1998). These ideas sum up the experiences and probable ambitions of our salon trainee but not our college trainee, who is only ever intending to be a 'fixed-term' member of the college-based Community of Hairdressing Practice, and only because they want to be able to gain access to a separate CoP – one based in a salon, a position of employment within the profession – after finishing at college. What is happening here is that our college trainee can only gain entry to one CoP – the salon – *after* finishing their college course. Put another way, our trainee can only gain entry to the salon CoP after the successful negotiation of the **peripheral trajectory** of the college-based CoP. Their entry into one CoP relies entirely on their completion of their time in another. Having completed their studies at college and with their certificates safely received, they can then enter the world of work.

Interlude: theoretical plug-ins

Our college-based trainee illustrates very neatly a key concept within CoP theory that was originally proposed not by Jean Lave or Etienne Wenger, but by Jay Lemke. Lemke, a professor at City University in New York, started out as a physicist before becoming interested in science education more broadly. As one of the wider group of researchers and writers working with social practice theories of learning, he was an early commentator on Lave and Wenger's original work. One of the problems that he identified with CoP theory was: what if mastery of the practice in one community depended on having first gained a level of mastery in a different one? What happens within a community when there is no expectation of full participation for some members, and where hierarchies (the obvious one for the purposes of our analysis is the student–teacher hierarchy) will therefore never be challenged? Lemke's solution (1997) was to propose the simple and elegant idea that sometimes membership of one CoP would only be available to people who had been members of another CoP first. Lemke's idea is a good example of a theoretical plug-in. In computing, a plug-in is a piece of software that adds a new feature to an existing computer application. For example: during lockdown I (like many other people) held lots of meetings on Zoom, so I downloaded a plug-in that lets me schedule a Zoom call from within Microsoft Outlook. Here, we can use 'plug-in' to refer to a new theoretical element that allows our main theory to do some new things that otherwise it would not be able to do. Just as with the computer software, though, our theoretical plug-in needs to be *compatible* with our main theory: sometimes plug-ins are poorly chosen or applied and this leads to theoretical incompatibilities. We shall discuss this in more detail in Chapter 3.

Both of our trainees learn in the same way – through Legitimate Peripheral Participation – but within different CoPs, therefore. Whether the CoP is based around a training salon in a further education college or a high street salon where NVQ assessors will come and visit, LPP works the same. Just so long as the practices made available to our two trainees are authentic and legitimate aspects of the work of the community, then learning will happen. Our trainees will pick up the language and habits of the community. They will be shown how the tools and processes of the community work. Old-timers and experts will demonstrate techniques and processes, guide them when they get stuck, and answer their questions. At first, they will try out simple tasks, and over time as their confidence grows and their expertise and understanding develops, they will be given the opportunity to do more complicated, more taxing activities. They will, by necessity, learn the language of the CoP through repeated conversations and learn the habits of the CoP through repeated actions. And as opportunity and interest allow, they might move across to other CoPs within the constellation over time. One trainee might decide that they want to specialise in bridal hair design and the other might want to specialise in fantasy hair design – and so they will travel across the constellation of hairdressing CoPs in order to do so.

What our two trainees will learn will become more complex, more technically demanding, richer and more esoteric over time. But *how* they learn these things – irrespective of their future specialisms – remains the same, and that goes for the hairdressing tutors in FE colleges learning how to be tutors, the workplace assessors learning how to be assessors, and the trainees and teachers in any other part of a further education college or adult education centre. They – we – are always learning, all of the time, at varying speeds, in different locations, for different reasons, with different people, drawing on a variety of resources and tools, engaging in all kinds of conversations, and always through **legitimate peripheral participation**. Learning is *never* a solitary, individual activity. How can it be? Learning always needs other people, either directly when we share a space such as a workshop, training room, classroom, or library, or indirectly when we link with others via webpages, books, or podcasts. Sometimes it will involve instructors or trainers in formal positions, whilst at other times old-timers or experts without official roles as teachers will nonetheless help the novices within the CoP pick things up as they go along.

Learning – whether through LPP for newcomers or through practice for full members – always involves others. And it always involves learning whatever needs to be learned, whether or not it is 'theoretical' or 'practical' – distinctions that CoP theory reject because the idea of dividing things between the theoretical and the practical was mistaken in the first place. So-called 'academic' subjects are not 'harder' or 'more challenging' than so-called 'vocational' subjects: the only reason why people thought that (and why some still do) is because psychological research placed an emphasis on cognition 'in the mind' at the expense of everything else that makes a person who they are. The social theory of learning that CoPs rest on is not just about what can be stored in long-term memory or what mental schema can be constructed. It is about the whole person: who we are, what we do, how we speak and act, how we stand and move, how we hold tools, express ideas, link concepts, solve problems, and help each other along. Anybody who has worked in a college knows that there is more to learning than passing exams or completing portfolios (although, as we shall see in Chapter 7, these are still important). It is in the way our apprentices learn to speak, the way they hold their tools, the kinds of questions that they ask, the novel solutions that they employ, and the increasing fluency and ease with which they more confidently go about their work, that we can observe, hear, and witness that learning has been happening.

Some conclusions

In this second chapter, we have explored the concept of legitimate peripheral participation (LPP) – the way in which we explain how learning is made available to any newcomer to a Community of Practice (CoP): our examples in this chapter have come from just one context (hairdressing) but examples from other vocational and technical areas will be drawn on in subsequent chapters. We have explored the trajectories of CoP members in depth, and begun to think about how CoPs change over time, which makes every member a learner of some kind and which illustrates the social theory of learning that is integral to CoP theory. In the following chapter, we shall look at a number of different research articles, books, and book chapters, and see what they can tell us about the further and adult education sectors more broadly, from a CoP perspective. For now, the key message is to remember the centrality of learning within any community: without learning, there cannot be a Community of Practice.

References

Billett, S. (1998) Ontogeny and participation in communities of practice: a socio-cognitive view of adult development. *Studies in the Education of Adults* 30 (1) 21–34. doi:10.1080/02660830.1998.11730670.

Billett, S. (2007) Including the missing subject: placing the personal within the community. In Hughes, J., Jewson, N. and Unwin, L. (eds.) *Communities of Practice: Critical Perspectives.* London: Routledge. 55–67.

Chaiklin, S. and Lave, J. (eds.) (1996) *Understanding practice: Perspectives on activity and context.* Cambridge: Cambridge University Press.

Curzon, L.B. and Tummons, J. (2013) *Teaching in Further Education: an outline of principles and practice.* Seventh edition. London: Bloomsbury.

Handley, K., Sturdy, A., Fincham, R. and Clark T. (2006) Within and Beyond Communities of Practice: Making Sense of Learning Through Participation, Identity and Practice. *Journal of Management Studies*, 43 (3) 641–653. doi:10.1111/j.1467-6486.2006.00605.x.

Lave, J. (1988) *Cognition in Practice: Mind, Mathematics and Culture in Everyday Life.* Cambridge: Cambridge University Press.

Lave, J. and Wenger, E. (1991) *Situated Learning: Legitimate Peripheral Participation.* Cambridge: Cambridge University Press.

Lemke, J. (1997) Cognition, context and learning: a social semiotic perspective. In Kirshner, D. and Whitson, J. (eds.) *Situated Cognition: Social, Semiotic and Psychological Perspectives.* London: Lawrence Erlbaum. 37–56.

Tummons, J. (2018) *Learning architectures in higher education: beyond communities of practice.* London: Bloomsbury.

Wenger, E. (1998) *Communities of Practice: Learning, Meaning and Identity.* Cambridge: Cambridge University Press.

3 Communities of Practice in further and adult education

What can we learn from the research?

Introduction

In this third chapter, I am going to widen our horizons, and discuss the work done about CoPs by other researchers and writers. I am not conducting a wide-ranging review of the literature. Nor am I setting out to list and then dismantle CoP-based papers written by others that I have found to be insufficiently thorough in their use of the theory. Here – and throughout this entire book – I am wanting to focus on what can be done with CoP theory when it is used well, not on what people have done when they have used it in a cursory fashion, when they have misunderstood elements of the theory, or when they write about CoPs without having read Lave and Wenger and/or Wenger first. There are two strands to this chapter, therefore. The first is to look at some examples of CoP work that are rooted within the further and adult education sectors; and the second is to look at examples of research that solve some of the problems that are present within CoP theory.

Drawing on, and moving away from, Lave and/or Wenger

Jean Lave and Etienne Wenger weren't working in a vacuum when they first coined the term 'communities of practice'. They were part of a larger group of researchers and writers working in a broader field, all with their own particular perspectives or 'takes' on learning as a social, not psychological, process. Following the publication of *Situated Learning*, these – and other – researchers soon started to pick up on the notion of the Community of Practice in order to inform their own writing in turn. Many examples of such work appeared before Wenger's *Communities of Practice* was published (Chaiklin and Lave, 1996; Kirshner and Whitson, 1997; Wertsch et al., 1995). Some of it predates the publication of *Situated Learning* (Rogoff and Lave, 1984), not least Lave's (1988) work *Cognition in Practice* (discussed in the preceding chapter). Subsequently, both Lave and Wenger have travelled separate paths. Wenger's later work, including reworked models of CoPs, have been applied to corporate and business contexts (Wenger et al., 2002). Lave's later work has seen her focus once again on her ethnographic research into different forms of apprenticeship learning (Lave, 1996, 2011). It is fascinating to see how the creators of the CoP

DOI: 10.4324/9781003252566-3

model have left it behind in some respects (Barton and Tusting, 2005), although it does make things rather difficult for those of us who still use it. Should we use the 'original' version from Wenger (1998), which feels more academic, or the 'revised' version from Wenger et al. (2002), which is more corporate? Should we set the idea of CoPs to one side and instead focus on Legitimate Peripheral Participation, remembering that in the first book, Lave and Wenger (1991: 42) described a CoP as a 'largely intuitive notion'? And what about the other ingredients that a number of writers have added to the CoP mix during the past three decades, or the additional research contexts and sites to which other researchers have taken the idea of the CoP?

The answers to questions such as these – perhaps inevitably – is: 'it depends'. There are a few different factors to think about. Take the discussion between Wenger's two versions of CoPs (although we should remember that the later version was in fact a collaborative work). If we were to do a search of business and management studies journals (I have done this, I should point out) we would find that the 2002 version of CoPs, which focusses more on how organisations can use a CoP approach for knowledge transfer and innovation in order to be more economically competitive, is the one most commonly used. The earlier 1998 version is more often – although not exclusively – used in education studies and sociology journals. And it is the version that this book rests on. At the same time, it is far from uncommon for a book chapter or a journal paper (I am not including professional newsletters or blog posts here because they are not peer reviewed) to talk about CoPs without properly defining or discussing them at all. On occasions such as this, the idea of the CoP is taken for granted but never properly explored, and this leads to a lack of theoretical precision, blunting the tools contained within the CoP toolbox. An author might be telling us that they are writing about a particular aspect of CoPs, or about a constellation of CoPs, but without seriously engaging with the literature, their use of specialist concepts and terms is unhelpful and lacks rigour. And just because a chapter or article contains references to Wenger's work, it doesn't mean that the author has put that work to good use: citations do not always equate to robust reading (Lang and Canning, 2010).

What this all means is that for either the researcher or the practitioner, reading around the subject (always recommended) is a course of action that needs to be carried out both carefully and critically, and how it gets done will depend on the job that we have set out to do. An exhaustive survey of CoP research would mean having to read everything – or certainly everything that fits the aims and scope of our survey. A *systematic review* is a particular approach to reading the research literature, in order to generate answers to new questions, which might require us to read everything that mentions 'Community of Practice' for us to then evaluate. After this, we might divide the literature between articles that use the 1998 model on the one hand, and the 2002 model on the other, for example. Or we might decide to undertake a more tightly focussed analysis that looks at how the CoP framework is currently being applied – a *state-of-the-art* review. We might want to think about how CoPs are being explored in specific contexts such as clinical education. To do this, we would, when conducting our review of the literature, search for papers that discuss the professional learning of nurses from a CoP context, or even how the concept of the Community of Practice is defined within health education research more broadly (Buckley et al., 2019; Thrysoe et al., 2012). Alternatively, we might instead consider the ways in which the theoretical basis of CoPs is being discussed, revised, or expanded. For such an inquiry, we can look for research papers and books that employ additional theoretical perspectives that might shed light on particular elements of CoP theory.

It is hoped that people who read this book will go on to explore further examples from the literature and perhaps also conduct their own empirical research. In so doing, looking across a wide range of sources is essential. But this process of reading will need to include the primary sources – *Situated Learning* and especially *Communities of Practice* – if it is to be taken seriously. After reading these, the wider body of literature falls into place, and the researcher can look for examples of how CoP theory has been used by others to inform research, challenge ideas, and operationalise the concepts set out by Lave and/or Wenger in a critical manner.

This chapter aims to provide a contribution to the wider reading. It is by no means exhaustive – a really extensive review of the literature would require a much longer book than this one. Nor is it critical in the sense that I am seeking to critique and argue against the notion of the CoP. Instead, I address two overlapping concerns. Our first concern is to consider literature that provides a *proof of concept* for CoPs – articles or chapters that show the CoP framework being put to good use in order to explore educational and training contexts that are aligned to the focus of this book: the further and adult education sector. In some instances, this empirical work helps in the generation of new theoretical insights. Consequently, our second concern (sometimes overlapping with the first) is to briefly discuss these and other authors who have put forward ideas or theories that usefully *expand* on CoP theory in ways that we might in turn apply to our own future research and scholarship.

Before we proceed, the limitations of the wider available literature are worth noting. The further and adult education sectors are, generally, under-researched in the UK in comparison to schools and universities. Within the research that is published, papers that focus on Communities of Practice are far outnumbered by papers that focus on *policy* (to pick just one example from the wider field of education research). So in order for our analysis to proceed, we need to draw on research from outside the UK. In the discussion that follows, I have used empirical research from both Australia and New Zealand for the simple reason that in both of these countries the technical and vocational sectors are comparable to what we find in the UK and we can, therefore, *translate* the findings from these studies into a UK context whilst the UK based studies travel in the opposite direction (Atkins and Tummons, 2017).

Putting Communities of Practice theory to work

The elasticity of CoP theory – assuming it is being carefully and critically used – means that our discussion can travel across a variety of contexts, encompassing nurses and healthcare professionals in Scotland, museum and gallery educators in England, modern apprentices in New Zealand, and teachers of floor- and wall-tiling courses in Australia, with the insights from specific contexts such as these nonetheless capable of generating conclusions that reinforce findings from elsewhere.

The research conducted by Wendy Mayne and colleagues offers a context for CoP-based work that is immediately recognisable – a partnership between a university and a network of further education colleges established in order to deliver courses in nursing and healthcare (Mayne et al., 2015). The CoP that is discussed in the paper brought together both university and college-based staff in order to enrich understandings of relevant professional learning and practice across the two sectors with a particular focus on *progression* from FE to HE for students. I would suggest that this constitutes a form of **boundary crossing**, although this is one element of CoP theory that they do not use in the paper. Instead, Mayne et al. focus on three other key concepts. First, they focus on learning as being – and needing to be – **meaningful** and rooted in practice. Second, they foreground the importance of CoPs as places not only to share knowledge and practice but also to generate new forms of both. And finally, they rework the **novice–expert** relationship in terms of academic–practitioner and mentor–mentee. Using this framework to inform their empirical research, Mayne et al. generate a series of useful conclusions. For students (novices), findings relate to the importance of sharing practice through experience, and the expectations that they have of the progression from FE to HE. For staff (experts), findings highlight the importance of curriculum alignment across institutions, and the similarities and differences between assessment and feedback practices between FE and HE settings. Mayne et al. acknowledge the relatively narrow empirical basis of their work, and their use of CoP theory in exploring these findings is rather restricted, but their conclusions are nonetheless noteworthy. The place of assessment and feedback within a CoP is complex and we shall return to this in Chapter 7.

Steve Herne's research into the work of educators in museums and galleries explores similar themes of movement across different spaces and places, but with a more explicit application of Wenger's concepts of **boundary objects** and **events** – the materials and practices that happen at the margins of CoPs and allows travel between them (discussed in more depth in Chapter 6). Herne (2006) imagines a **constellation** of Communities of Practice consisting of museums, galleries, and schools, and seeks to explore the ways in which the stuff of galleries and museums is made available and accessible to schools – to both the teachers who organise the visits and work with gallery educators, and to the students. For Herne, the **boundary objects** are the booklets, teacher packs, websites, and suchlike that travel from a museum to a school, where the students – and teachers, if necessary – can start to get to know about the stuff of the museum beforehand. Subsequently, these same boundary objects can be carried along by the student and teachers on the day of their visit, to help them find their way around and make sense of whatever it is that they have come to see and to study, and then revise from them once more when back in school. Additionally – and importantly – the booklets and websites allow a kind of marginal or (better) **peripheral** access to the stuff of the museum even for people who cannot actually go there in person. The museum educators and teachers take on a **brokering** role, creating bridges between the two CoPs of museum and school in order to help the students – the **visitors** – make the most of their study trip. And whilst the teacher may possess experience and expertise relating to the stuff of the museum, the presence of the educator provides an additional element of **authenticity**.

A third and very different kind of work across CoPs is explored by Frank Sligo and colleagues in their account of the literacy learning undertaken by young adult apprentices on the New Zealand New Apprenticeship programme (Sligo et al., 2019). The problematic issues that Sligo et al. explore are familiar ones (and certainly familiar to me, when reflecting on my experiences in the three FE colleges that I worked in): how best can apprentices who are preparing to enter a specific trade or industry be encouraged to engage with the compulsory literacy components of their programmes of learning? Perhaps unsurprisingly, Sligo et al. found that the apprentices whom they studied were reluctant to engage in the bookwork that both they and their employers and workplace trainers perceived as being 'divorced from the realities of the workplace' (2019: 117). For the apprentices, any literacy component to their studies only made sense in terms of the workplaces that they aspired to join – workplaces where oracy is used as much, if not more often, than literacy. Remembering that any industry or trade has a particular way of talking and writing as part of the **shared repertoire** of that CoP (discussed in Chapter 1), it perhaps comes as no surprise that the only kinds of literacy that the apprentices were willing to put effort into were those that could be meaningfully applied to the workplace, and then only if a spoken-word alternative was not available. And whilst the wider, even emancipatory, benefits of literacy were an obvious element of the literacy tutors' professional identities, the apprentices saw any additional literacy components as being imposed on them unnecessarily. The shift in **identity** (a key component of learning within any CoP) came not from the apprentices, but from the literacy tutors who realised over time that their social justice goals were best served not by making the apprentices become 'more literate' but by helping them complete their apprenticeships alongside more limited, work-specific literacy learning, so that they could enter the industrial CoPs of their choice.

The focus shifts away from apprentices and towards teachers in the fourth paper that I wish to discuss, by David Boud and Heather Middleton, who explore a number of different contexts of workplace learning in Australia. One of the four cases discussed is of teachers of floor and wall tiling who are having to adjust their teaching practice to cope with a number of changes – to the curriculum that they teach, to the increased use of ICTs in the teaching workplace, and to product changes within the tiling industry (Boud and Middleton, 2003). Here, it is the tiling students who are positioned as members of CoPs that are tied to the industry that they are a part of, whilst the extent to whether or not the teachers constitute a CoP is less certain (although I would argue that they are). There are several overlaps between the teaching context – the tilers attend training on a day release basis – and the work context that echo the **boundary** work and cross-border traffic by **brokers** that appear in the paper by Herne (2006). The students tell the teachers what their employers think about the training that they are receiving. They also provide information to the teachers about new products. Trade representatives and specialists visit the training site and provide demonstrations of new materials and tools, and there is also informal social contact between the teachers and the working tilers. Boud and Middleton are more circumspect in their use of CoP theory, and argue that the teachers – as well as some of the other workplace learning cases that they explore – exhibit some but not all of the characteristics of a Community of Practice. They also extend CoP theory through referring to the work of the educational sociologist Basil Bernstein. Bernstein's framework of curriculum and knowledge was based in part on the organization of bodies of knowledge into a curriculum (Bernstein, 1990). The *framing* of any curriculum (Bernstein's research was based in schools) is a way of considering how much, or how little, freedom of movement the following of that curriculum affords to the teacher and to the pupils. Borrowing this idea, Boud and Middleton suggest (all too briefly, perhaps, as it is an interesting idea) that CoPs might be considered as being either *tightly framed* in the case of the tilers, whose practice is focussed around a specific body of work, or *weakly framed* in the case of the teachers of tiling, whose practice is more varied and changeable.

Boud and Middleton (2003) hint at a useful extension for CoP theory. In a similar vein, the research done by Alison Fuller and colleagues (Fuller et al., 2005) seeks to provide a more extensively critical appraisal of the concept of **Legitimate Peripheral Participation** and to evaluate how it might be used to explore workplace learning. Their research as based on a *comparative case study* of Modern Apprentices in the UK steel industry. At one of the research sites, the apprenticeship programme was highly structured, with a year of college-based study followed by three years in the workplace with the opportunity to move between different departments on a rota basis, attending college on a day-release basis. The programme was looser at the second site, and the company was using the Modern Apprenticeship framework to resolve recruitment shortages: here, apprentices spent the bulk of their time on the shop floor, with their on-the-job training augmented by half-day courses. The provision at the third site was looser still: here, there was no off-job training, and the Modern Apprentices were effectively treated as employees in a specific part of the company. Drawing on this as well as other research findings, Fuller and colleagues offer four limitations of Lave and/or Wenger's work, but two of these are, I suggest, in themselves limited by only a partial use of CoP theory. Firstly, they argue that the concept of LPP is only able to account for the learning of apprentices or established workers who are moving to a new department – a new CoP – for example. But this argument fails to consider the ways in which CoPs change over time, and that such changes always generate new practices and therefore new things to learn (as discussed in Chapter 2). If the **joint enterprise** of a CoP shifts, then even the experts – the 'old-timers' – become a bit more peripheral as they too now have new things to learn. Secondly, Fuller et al. suggest that Lave and Wenger focus too much on what a member – a worker – gets *from* the CoP and not enough on what the worker brings *to* the CoP. However, this argument does not recognise the notion of **multimembership** and of how people can carry ideas and experience with them as they travel between communities (as we shall discuss in Chapter 6) and as such can be put to one side. The other two arguments raised deserve serious attention: one is that Lave and Wenger are overly dismissive of formal teaching and of pedagogy, and we shall briefly return to this later in this chapter, and more extensively in Chapter 4; the other is that the theory lacks the tools for thinking about how power is enacted within a CoP, and we shall discuss this in Chapter 5.

Bridging the empirical and the theoretical

The papers by Boud and Middleton (to some degree) and Fuller et al. (in a more extensive manner) exemplify the kinds of arguments that I am seeking to contribute to in this book: arguments and lines of analysis that draw on a good empirical grounding in order to advance theoretical points of view that have firm foundations in research. As well as providing meaningful examples of CoP theory at work that are relevant to teachers and trainers in the further and adult education sectors, they also exhibit a critical approach that leads to new possibilities for CoP theory more broadly. They contribute to an important process of *theory building* (Kettley, 2010) – the careful accumulation of research and writing that can reinforce and sometimes improve on a particular perspective or approach. Theory building is important because it can help us to test out or snag the particular approach that we are interested in. If we decide to adopt a theoretical or conceptual framework without question or hesitation, and without careful and critical reading (it doesn't have to be CoP theory, of course, as there are lots of others), then we run the risk of misusing and/or misunderstanding the theory in question – and in the literature on Communities of Practice, this happens quite a lot (Curzon and Tummons, 2013; Tight, 2015; Tummons, 2014, 2018). A second risk is that we find ourselves subscribing to theories or concepts that are of dubious quality with a consequent risk of negative impact, and this might be in terms of our research or our professional practice: the example of *learning styles* theory being the standout example of a bad theory that has led to distortions in pedagogy, despite being extensively debunked (Coffield et al., 2004; Curzon and Tummons, 2013).

Happily, whilst learning styles theories now mostly reside in the dustbin of history, CoP theory continues to evolve in a more robust as well as more constructive fashion. As discussed in Chapter 1, part of this evolution has come about through the ongoing work done – although now separately – by Lave and Wenger, developments that are welcomed by some although critiqued by others (Hughes, 2007). The papers discussed above from Boud and Middleton (2003) and Fuller et al. (2005) also provide further developments of the concept on the back of robust empirical research. And there are many other books, papers, and chapters that seek to move CoP theory on, sometimes to plug a perceived gap, sometimes to add more detail or finesse to an existing aspect of the theory. Some of this literature is once again based on research but with a primary focus on theoretical rather than empirical contributions, whereas other examples from the literature do not discuss primary research at all, but rest entirely on arguments derived from theoretical and conceptual sources.

Building on Communities of Practice theory

Stephen Billett's exploration of the workplace learning of hairdressers (referred to in the previous chapter) forms just one element of his wider research into sites of workplace learning that have ranged from customer service to manufacturing, drawing on a range of theories including CoPs (Billett, 1998, 2002, 2007), and his statement on Communities of Practice theory – that they are 'far more often more popularly endorsed than critically appraised' (Billett, 2007: 55) – is one that I share. Billett has written extensively about processes of learning, as distinct from the social and cultural spaces within which learning happens, and as such offers useful tools for thinking about learning through **Legitimate Peripheral Participation**, foregrounding the context or *situated nature* of learning through LPP. He describes how, at one of the salons included in his research, the hairdressers' work was differentiated not in terms of the individual client – that is to say, one hairdresser attended to one client – but in terms of the complexity of the individual task that was being carried out. As such, he observed considerable degrees of movement by hairdressers between the clients in the salon, as one hairdresser would take over from another as the work on a client became more demanding. Adding further complexity to the practices of the salon, the (male) proprietor insisted that all of the hairdressers worked in silence without talking to the clients, leading the hairdressers to develop their own language of gestures and hand signals in order to communicate.

How are we to make sense of the learning through LPP that is to be found in a Community of Hairdressing Practice such as this? Certainly, any notion that the learning from this CoP might be in any way straightforwardly transferable to another can be easily dismissed, highlighting the *situatedness* of the practice. For Billett (2007: 65), this closeness to practice is the key contribution of Lave and Wenger's work. At the same time, Billett observed that the hairdressers, notwithstanding the restrictions placed upon them by the proprietor, continued to demonstrate forms of expertise and skill that they had brought with them from elsewhere. Here, he draws on earlier work (Billett, 1998) in proposing that expertise (whether in hairdressing or anything else) requires the apprentice to have access to not only 'everyday' routine but also non-routine practices. Routine activities will be enough for the person who is happy to remain a **peripheral participant**, but non-routine activities allow for the generation of the expertise that the **full participant** requires. He also proposes a third classification for participation – the *principal participant* (Billett, 1998: 30) – to describe those members of a CoP who may not be full members in terms of expertise in the practice, but nonetheless are able to determine the extent of other peoples' participation.

Billett's research chimes with the original work of Lave and Wenger (1991) and Wenger (1998) in that he too is interested in exploring instances of workplace learning where there is no formal instruction or curriculum in order to allow for the novice or apprentice to receive a formal qualification. By contrast, Alison Fuller and Lorna Unwin, in their extensive research on Modern Apprenticeships in the UK (as referred to above), are explicitly focussed on more formal structures for learning, and have sought to build on the concept of LPP in order to do so (Fuller and Unwin, 2003). In order to do so, they draw on a further theoretical framework – *activity theory* (Engeström et al., 1999). Activity theory is arguably not all that familiar to practitioners (as distinct from researchers) in further and adult education (Curzon and Tummons, 2013), although one of the 'ancestors' of activity theory – Vygotsky, who coined the concept of the Zone of Proximal Development – is perhaps better known. In developing his theory of learning, Engeström sought, amongst other things, to resolve what he perceived as a problem with Legitimate Peripheral Participation – namely, that LPP could not account for the unexpected or contradictory directions that learners might choose to follow (Engeström, 1999).

Building on Engeström's work, Fuller and Unwin suggest that depending on the kinds of CoPs that apprentices are able to participate in and the nature of that participation, their learning will be either *expansive* or *restrictive* (Fuller and Unwin, 2003: 411). Thus, expansive learning would require meaningful engagement for the Modern Apprentice within a CoP in such a way that there were no restrictions on participation, opportunities for knowledge as well as competence-based qualifications, a focus on the development of the individual as well as the needs of the organisation, and opportunities to learn from other CoPs in order to develop a breadth of experience and knowledge. Restrictive learning, by contrast, would be characterised by limited opportunity, an instrumental approach to obtaining qualifications, a lack of concern for the development of the individual in favour of the requirements of the organisation, and limited access to other CoPs. Thinking back to the paper by Fuller et al. (2005), which we explored earlier and which rests on the same research, we can see clearly that the first of the three research sites offered opportunities for expansive learning, with the two other sites exhibiting more restrictive characteristics.

A further contribution to the ways in which we might understand Legitimate Peripheral Participation and the position held by novices within a Community of Practice is made by James Brooks and colleagues in their ethnography of 'Northern Fire' (a pseudonym), part of the UK Fire and Rescue Service.

Through exploring the role played by novices within these CoPs – and the impact of a lack of novices due to recruitment freezes caused by budget cuts – Brooks et al. (2020) both illustrate and expand several of the key concepts originally proposed by Lave and Wenger and Wenger. An example of how Brooks et al. put CoP theory to work is found in their discussion of the important role played by narrative – by telling stories – within the CoP. The history of any CoP is an important resource for learning and for identity formation (Wenger, 1998: 83–4): within Northern Fire, the stories told to the novices by the old-timers during periods of down-time between calls or more formal training activities such as drill training (exercises such as practicing different techniques for ensuring that a building has been evacuated) were not merely aspects of the culture of the service, but also vehicles for sharking experiences and knowledge. But of equal importance to the CoP were the affordances for learning generated by having novices within the service. For the old-timers, the presence of the novices was a prompt for reflection and for revisiting well-established aspects of practice, even for keeping up with the novices, but also for acquiring new and different techniques such as the Cleveland Load – a way of packing firehoses in a very tight manner so as to make them more capable of being carried by just one person, and of particular value when working in high-rise buildings (Brooks et al., 2020: 1055). According to this account, learning within a CoP is a *multi-directional* phenomenon, involving both novices and experts alike: the novices learn from, amongst other things, the stories and experiences of the experts in just the same way that the experts learn about new techniques from the novices and are encouraged to reflect on their own past learning through, and as a consequence of, their interactions with the novices. Irrespective of the direction of travel, the learning is the same.

There are two elements of CoP theory at work here, although only one is foregrounded. The foregrounded element is LPP: it is not the case that Lave and Wenger (1991) and later Wenger (1998) argue that learning only happens in only one direction as the newcomer travels along their **trajectory** towards expertise and experience; rather, it is the case that they simply fail to explore in full the implications of their ideas. The research into Northern Fire plugs this gap, making explicit an otherwise tacit aspect of CoP theory, and providing an empirical basis to reinforce their analysis. The second element of CoP theory at work that is not present in the paper is that of **change** within a CoP as a factor in generating new opportunities and/or requirements for learning (Wenger, 1998), as discussed in Chapter 2. From this standpoint, the new ways of doing things that the novices bring with them constitute a change in practice and therefore a change in learning for all members of the community, whatever their location along their trajectories.

Interlude: making sure that your upgrades are compatible

In the preceding chapter, we took a brief interlude concerning theoretical plug-ins. It is now time to explore this issue more critically.

One of the ways in which education researchers engage in theory building is through drawing on two – sometimes more – theories at the same time in order to see how they might complement each other and in turn shed new light on the problem being explored. Boud and Middleon (2003) borrow from Bernstein's *curriculum theory* in their analysis, and Fuller and Unwin (2003) borrow from Engeström and *activity theory*. These combinations work because even though the two parts of each combination are of course different, they are nonetheless compatible because they share some common ground in terms of their intellectual foundations.

Discussions about the philosophy of knowledge – what does it mean when we say that we know something? How is knowledge constructed or established? – are a common feature of academic discussions. Any FE professional who is also studying for a research degree will almost certainly have come across these discussions, which are grouped together under the label of *epistemology* – theory of knowledge. Different theoretical frameworks rest on different ideas about how the knowledge that contributes to those frameworks is put together in the first place. Or, to put it another way, different frameworks rest on different epistemologies. Lave and Wenger's anthropological work is based on a way of establishing knowledge about something – in their case, knowledge about apprentices and apprenticeship learning in a variety of contexts – that is very different from the way in which educational psychologists such as Thorndike (behaviourism), Gagné or Skinner (neobehaviourism), or Bruner (cognitivism). These are names that are found within the teacher-training curriculum for further and adult educators far more frequently than is the case for Lave and Wenger (Curzon and Tummons, 2013). Broadly speaking, psychology, as an academic discipline, rests on a different way of establishing knowledge than anthropology: they have different epistemologies.

Knowledge exists within the world around us – in books, in podcasts, in what people say and what they do – and so in order to think about knowledge – about epistemology – we also have to think about the world that the knowledge is a part of: these discussions are grouped together under the label of *ontology* – theory of being and reality. Ontology shapes epistemology – the one informs the other. For the psychologist, 'intelligence' is an inherent aspect of human cognition that needs to be measured and codified: that way, we can explore what learning is – from one particular perspective, and then generalise our conclusions to include the whole population. For the anthropologist, 'intelligence' is an idea that has been drawn up and then used by people, and it is how and why they did this, and what it implies, that is of interest. Instead of measuring 'intelligence', they would want to know why we are talking about it in the first place. The psychologist and the anthropologist have very different views about how the world works – they occupy different ontologies.

When we are theory building by combining different theoretical perspectives, therefore, we need to ensure that our two components are compatible with each other. They need to have epistemological and ontological compatibility if they are going to be able to work together, in just the same way that a freshly downloaded app needs to be compatible with the operating system of your tablet or phone: if you are running an incompatible OS, then the app won't work. This is why Engeström, and Lave and Wenger can be brought together.

New additions to the CoP toolbox

Broadly speaking, we can recognise two kinds of CoP addition (once more allowing for a little overlap between them). On the one hand we have got additions that are based on further extensive empirical research – for example, Billett's (1998) research leading to the introduction of the concept of the *principal participant* within a CoP. On the other hand, we have got additions based on empirical work but very much shaped by other compatible theoretical frameworks – for example, the use of elements of Engeström's theories by Fuller and Unwin (2003). What follows is a brief account of some other additions that might be useful for our inquiry into CoPs in further and adult education and training. One or two of these authors have already been mentioned in the book up to this point, and the others are new arrivals.

The role of language within a CoP

Karin Tusting (2005) has focussed on Wenger's concept of **negotiation of meaning** (Wenger, 1998: 52). In order to make meaning within a CoP, to begin to not only learn but also understand things, Wenger proposes that a two-way process – a negotiation – is at work between our practice – our actions, behaviours, speech – within a CoP on the one hand, and the ways in which the stuff of the CoP – the tools, routines, materials, habits – are invented, used, or adapted. For Tusting, this is an element of CoP theory that requires further enhancement (Tusting, 2005). Her approach is to think more deeply about the role of language within this negotiation of meaning. She acknowledges that Wenger does recognise that language forms part of the process, but goes further and suggests that if we really want to know more about the negotiation of meaning within a CoP, we need to use a more sophisticated theoretical approach to language than Wenger does – an approach that looks at language in relation to all of the other social practices at work within the community. Tusting proposes using approaches derived from *linguistics* – the systematic study of human language. In this way we can explore how language is used to express personal identity, to represent social or power structures. Or we might consider how different types or *genres* of text carry different meanings for different members within a CoP.

CoPs, and gender

Gender theory explores what is feminine and/or masculine – or neither – in social contexts and behaviour and these might range from educational curricula to the experiences of people at work, and this concept can be traced back to the end of the nineteenth century (Ritzer and Stepnisky, 2018). From this perspective, Carrie Paechter has asked the question: what if masculinities or femininities are Communities of Practice? She pluralises these in order to reflect that being feminine and/or masculine, or neither, can take different forms depending on cultural context, geography, age, and so forth (**Paechter, 2003**). If part of what being feminine or being masculine is relies on learning about them in a social context, then perhaps CoP theory can provide an additional tool for inquiry? Paechter illustrates her argument through using several key elements of CoP theory. For example, if we accept that being feminine or being masculine are changeable according to social or cultural contexts – that there are different 'kinds' of both and these change over time and across social spaces – then we can think about the **boundaries** that might wrap around femininity or masculinity as a CoP – boundaries can change but that will always nonetheless welcome some people but exclude others. Similarly, Wenger's ideas about **identity** – which is part of the process of learning through **Legitimate Peripheral Participation** – are discussed in terms of practice: for example, certain forms of masculinity are formed through practices related to competitive sports and this allows young men to both form their own identities and also project or display that identity to others within the community (Paechter, 2003: 74).

Legitimate peripheral participation, and illegitimate peripheral participation

In the preceding chapter we explored **Legitimate Peripheral Participation** (LPP) – the theory of learning that underpins any Community of Practice. In their original work, Lave and Wenger suggested that 'there may very well be no such thing as an "illegitimate peripheral participant". The form that the legitimacy of participation takes is [...] a crucial condition for learning' (1991: 35). Harris and Shelswell (2005) beg to differ, however, basing their conclusions on research into adult basic skills provision at an Open Learning Centre in Wales. Harris and Shelswell describe how, over time, a minority of the members of this adult basic education CoP would try to shape or influence how the community would work, or to dominate group discourse within the community, by drawing on previous experiences or skills that were significant aspects of the participant's identity in the past but which are outside the practice of the current community. On such occasions, when members would attempt to 'shoehorn' such elements of their identity and past practice into the community – often causing friction and/or resistance from other members – a form of disruption or conflict emerged. For Harris and Shelswell, this was a form of peripheral participation that fell outside the joint enterprise of the CoP – it was illegitimate (2005: 168).

New patterns of multi-membership

During the plug-ins interlude in the preceding chapter, I referred to a CoP theory workaround proposed by Jay Lemke (1997) in order to resolve one problematic aspect of CoP theory. Lemke's argument – really, a simple observation, but a crucial one – was laid out as follows. Imagine someone wanting to become a medical doctor: the CoP of qualified, working doctors is clearly separate in clearly observed ways from the CoP of 'apprentice' doctors (as it were). You can't become a doctor simply by 'picking things up as you go and learning on the job', even if you do manage to convince some of the old-timers that you have an aptitude for performing minor surgical procedures. In order to explain how people get to train as doctors, we need to maintain the CoP model whilst at the same time acknowledging that many forms of formal learning do not neatly fit the learning through practice apprenticeship model that Lave and Wenger (1991) absorb within the LPP framework. Lemke's solution was simple: what if membership of one CoP required prior membership of a different, related, CoP? Before joining the medical CoP, you would first be required to navigate successfully the medical education CoP. The ways in which people can trace their memberships across multiple CoPs, as well as the ways in which CoPs might work together, were explored in depth by Wenger (1998), who over time has directed much of his attention to the exploration of this wider landscape of CoPs (Wenger-Trayner et al., 2015), and we shall return to this discussion in Chapter 6.

Some conclusions

We will come across a small number of other new items for the CoP toolbox as this book proceeds. In the following chapter we are going to think about how to reconcile CoP theory with formal pedagogy, something that Lave and Wenger categorically rejected. In Chapter 5, we shall discuss how inequalities of power and status within CoPs can be made sense of. In Chapter 6, we will return to the role of artefacts, texts, and objects – aspects of the **shared repertoire** – of CoPs. And in Chapter 7 we will think about how assessment and feedback – unavoidable aspects of practice within the further and adult education sectors – can be included within CoPs. But with all of these extras in the mix, we might ask ourselves: why are we even bothering with CoP theory if it needs revising and adding to from the start? It's a fair question, but one that should not put us off. The first answer is: lots of similar theoretical frameworks evolve over time and thanks to additional contributors, in just the same way that COP theory is in itself one of a number of related post-Vygotskian theories (as discussed above). The second answer is: so long as these new additions are compatible with CoP theory, then it's fine. And the third answer is: so long as we use our theories – 'original' CoP theory plus additions – carefully and critically, explaining with care the steps that we take in our research and writing, then we will be best placed to present our ideas as being robust and reliable – qualities that are vitally important for ongoing research within the further and adult education sectors.

References

Atkins, L. and Tummons, J. (2017) Professionalism in vocational education: international perspectives. *Research in Post-Compulsory Education* 22 (3) 355–369. doi:10.1080/13596748.2017.1358517.

Barton, D. and Tusting, K. (eds.) (2005) *Beyond Communities of Practice: Language, Power and Social Context.* Cambridge: Cambridge University Press.

Bernstein, B. (1990) *Class Codes and Control IV: The structuring of pedagogic discourse.* London: Routledge.

Billett, S. (1998) Ontogeny and participation in communities of practice: a socio-cognitive view of adult development. *Studies in the Education of Adults* 30 (1) 21–34. doi:10.1080/02660830.1998.11730670.

Billett, S. (2002) Workplace pedagogic practices: co-participation and learning. *British Journal of Educational Studies* 50 (4) 457–481. doi:10.1111/1467-8527.t01-2-00214.

Billett, S. (2007) Including the missing subject: placing the personal within the community. In Hughes, J., Jewson, N. and Unwin, L. (eds) *Communities of Practice: Critical Perspectives.* London: Routledge. 55–67.

Boud, D. and Middleton, H. (2003) Learning from others at work: communities of practice and informal learning. *Journal of Workplace Learning* 15 (5) 194–202. doi:10.1108/13665620310483895.

Brooks, J., Grugulis, I., and Cook, H. (2020) Rethinking situated learning: participation and communities in the UK fire and rescue service. *Work, Employment and Society* 34 (6) 1045–1061. doi:10.1177/0950017020913225.

Buckley, H., Steinert, Y., Regher, G. and Nimmon, L. (2019) When I say…community of practice. *Medical Education* 53 (8) 763–765. doi:10.1111/medu.13823.

Chaiklin, S. and Lave, J. (eds.) (1996) *Understanding practice: Perspectives on activity and context.* Cambridge: Cambridge University Press.

Coffield, F., Moseley, D., Hall, E. and Ecclestone, K. (2004) *Should We Be Using Learning Styles? What research has to say to practice.* London: Learning and Skills Research Centre.

Curzon, L. B. and Tummons, J. (2013) *Teaching in Further Education: an outline of principles and practice.* Seventh edition. London: Bloomsbury.

Engeström, Y. (1999) Activity theory and individual and social transformation. In Engeström, Y., Miettinen, R. and Punamäki, R-L. (eds.) *Perspectives on Activity Theory.* Cambridge: Cambridge University Press. 19–38.

Engeström, Y., Miettinen, R. and Punamäki, R-L. (eds.) (1999) *Perspectives on Activity Theory.* Cambridge: Cambridge University Press.

Fuller, A., Hodkinson, H., Hodkinson, P. and Unwin, L. (2005) Learning as peripheral participation in communities of practice: a re-assessment of key concepts in workplace learning. *British Educational Research Journal* 31 (1) 49–68. doi:10.1080/0141192052000310029.

Fuller, A. and Unwin, L. (2003) Learning as apprentices in then contemporary UK workplace: creating and managing expansive and restrictive participation. *Journal of Education and Work* 16 (4) 407–426. doi:10.1080/1363908032000093012.

Harris S. and Shelswell, N. (2005) *Moving beyond communities of practice in adult basic education.* In Barton, D. and Tusting, K. (eds.) *Beyond Communities of Practice: Language, Power and Social Context.* Cambridge: Cambridge University Press. 158–179.

Herne, S. (2006) Communities of practice in art and design and museum and gallery education. *Pedagogy, Culture and Society* 14 (1) 1–17. doi:10.1080/14681360500487512.

Hughes, J. (2007) *Lost in translation: communities of practice – the journey from academic model to practitioner tool.* In Hughes, J., Jewson, N. and Unwin, L. (eds.) *Communities of Practice: critical perspectives.* London: Routledge. 30–40.

Kettley, N. (2010) *Theory building in educational research.* London: Bloomsbury.

Kirshner, D. and Whitson, J. (eds.) (1997) *Situated Cognition: Social, Semiotic and Psychological Perspectives.* London: Lawrence Erlbaum Associates.

Lang, I. and Canning, R. (2010) The use of citations in educational research: the instance of the concept of 'situated learning'. *Journal of Further and Higher Education* 34 (2), 291–301. doi:10.1080/03098771003695924.

Lave, J. (1988) *Cognition in Practice: Mind, Mathematics and Culture in Everyday Life.* Cambridge: Cambridge University Press.

Lave, J. (1996) Teaching, as learning, in practice. *Mind, Culture and Activity* 3 (3) 149–164. doi:10.1207/s15327884mca0303_2.

Lave, J. (2011) *Apprenticeship in critical ethnographic practice.* Chicago: University of Chicago Press.

Lave, J. and Wenger, E. (1991) *Situated Learning: Legitimate Peripheral Participation.* Cambridge: Cambridge University Press.

Lemke, J. (1997) Cognition, context and learning: a social semiotic perspective. In Kirshner, D. and Whitson, J. (eds.) *Situated Cognition: Social, Semiotic and Psychological Perspectives.* London: Lawrence Erlbaum. 37–56.

Mayne, W., Andrew, N., Drury, C., Egan, I., Leitch, A. and Malone, M. (2015) 'There's more unites us than divides us!' A further and higher education community of practice in nursing. *Journal of Further and Higher Education* 39 (2) 163–179. doi:10.1080/0309877X.2013.817000.

Paechter, C. (2003) Masculinities and femininities as communities of practice. *Women's Studies International Forum* 26 (1) 69–77. doi:10.1016/S0277-5395(02)00356-4.

Ritzer, G. and Stepnisky, J. (2018) *Sociological Theory.* Tenth edition. London: Sage.

Rogoff, B. and Lave, J. (1984). *Everyday cognition: Its development in social context.* Cambridge, MA: Harvard University Press.

Sligo, F., Tilley, E., Murray, N., and Comrie, M. (2019) Community of practice versus community of readers: the literacy tutors' dilemma. *Journal of Vocational Education and Training* 71 (1) 108–125. doi:10.1080/13636820.2018.1464052.

Thrysoe, L., Hounsgaard, L., Dohn, N. and Wanger, L. (2012) Newly qualified nurses – experiences of interaction with members of a community of practice. *Nurse Education Today* 32 (5) 551–555. doi:10.1016/j.nedt.2011.07.008.

Tight, M. (2015) Theory application in higher education research: the case of communities of practice. *European Journal of Higher Education* 5 (2) 111–126. doi:10.1080/21568235.2014.997266.

Tummons, J. (2014). Learning architectures and communities of practice in higher education. In Huisman, J. and Tight, M. (eds) *Theory and Method in Higher Education Research* II. Bingley: Emerald Group Publishing Limited. 121–139.

Tummons, J. (2018) *Learning architectures in higher education: beyond communities of practice.* London: Bloomsbury.

Tusting, K. (2005) Language and Power in Communities of Practice. In Barton, D. and Tusting, K. (eds) *Beyond Communities of Practice: Language, Power and Social Context.* Cambridge: Cambridge University Press. 36–54.

Wenger, E. (1998) *Communities of Practice: Learning, Meaning and Identity.* Cambridge: Cambridge University Press.

Wenger, E., McDermott, R. and Snyder, W. (2002) *Cultivating Communities of Practice.* Boston: Harvard Business School Press.

Wenger-Trayner, E., Fenton-O'Creevy, M., Hutchinson, S., Kubiak, C. and Wenger-Trayner, B. (eds) (2015) *Learning in Landscapes of Practice: boundaries, identity and knowledgeability in practice-based learning.* London: Routledge.

Wertsch, J., Del Río, P. and Alvarez, A. (eds) (1995) *Sociocultural studies of mind.* Cambridge: Cambridge University Press.

4   Setting up a Learning Architecture

Introduction

In this fourth chapter, I am going to outline some of the key features of a Learning Architecture. This discussion will draw together several of the strands outlined in the preceding three chapters, but will also introduce a small number of components of CoP theory that we have yet to encounter. With reference to the more familiar world of curriculum theory, we will explore the ways in which a Community of Practice can be encouraged into being within the context of a formal educational establishment through establishing a Learning Architecture – a blueprint for a CoP.

The problem: where is the pedagogy in a Community of Practice?

The sheer diversity of the further and adult education sector is both a strength and a weakness – a diversity that is reflected even in the different terms and labels that have been used over time by government departments, funding agencies, and the like. We might pick and mix from: further and adult education; the lifelong learning sector; post-compulsory education and training; the learning and skills sector; work-based learning; the further education and skills sector. In some ways, the sector is best defined in terms of what it is not: it is not schools, and it is not universities. Any one of those labels nonetheless helps us to think about the diversity that we see every day, whether we are working in a large mixed economy further education college or in a small community-education class. Whether or not our students are part-time apprentices on day release, adults learning conversational English, or seventeen-year-olds studying for T levels, our professional practice will always require a commitment to a series of pedagogic principles that are increasingly discussed in terms of being *research-led* or *research-informed*. Pedagogy is at the heart of our professional practice as tutors, trainers, and lecturers (and I am deliberately ignoring variants such as andragogy or heutagogy because they cause more problems than they solve [Curzon and Tummons, 2013]).

Unfortunately for those of us who have, over the years, been inspired by Lave and Wenger's work, the very idea of any kind of mode of instruction – of

DOI: 10.4324/9781003252566-4

pedagogy – is anathema to the perspective on situated learning that they put forward:

> In a community of practice, there are no special forms of discourse aimed at apprentices or crucial to their centripetal movement toward full participation that correspond to the marked genres of the question-answer-evaluation format of classroom teaching, or the lecturing of college professors or midwife-training course instructors.
>
> (Lave and Wenger, 1991: 108)

For Lave and Wenger, the *pedagogy problem* (Tummons, 2018) is unambiguous. An apprentice does not/cannot learn from talking about the practice that they wish to engage with – that would simply mean that they are listening to talk about something rather than learning to talk about it themselves. The discourses of classroom teaching become an obstacle that gets in the way of the authentic – legitimate – practice that the community is about. This makes sense if we stick with four of the particular empirical examples of apprenticeship learning that Lave and Wenger's book rests on (1991: 65): tailors in Liberia (Lave's own ethnographic research), midwives in Mexico, quartermasters in the US Navy, and butchers in US supermarkets. It seems right to agree with Lave and Wenger that becoming part of one of these Communities of Practice (remembering that CoPs are not explicitly defined in their book) requires authentic induction into the practice in question, not formal learning within a school-based setting. But we still have to make sense of schools, colleges and universities. These formal educational structures are all around us and need to be understood. If a CoP – in the 'original' Lave and Wenger sense – is a vaguely defined but nonetheless 'non-formal-schooling' institution within which learning through LPP can be traced, then what kind of spaces are the classrooms or colleges that Lave and Wenger imply have no place within their theoretical frameworks? How can we get from tailors or butchers learning on the job, to day-release trainees blending workplace learning with classroom learning in a college?

Originally, and as we have already seen, a Community of Practice was a fairly undefined social formation, loosely imagined as a collection of people all sharing a particular expertise or craft. Within this conversation, the important role of specific forms of communication or specific kinds of tools and materials is briefly discussed but never unpacked to any great depth. Indeed, the relative slightness of the book as a whole has been a point of concern for several commentators. Not until we get to Wenger's later book do we find both a rich ethnographic account of the research on which the ideas are resting, and detailed explorations of the theoretical framework that emerge around that research. In their earlier book, Lave and Wenger were not interested in formal educational structures, and whilst the ethnographic research that Wenger wrote about in his later book – research in medical insurance claims processing – is very much situated in the world of work rather than the world of formal, institutional education and training, he does nonetheless expand on the theory in such a way as to imagine how it might be used to explore more formal processes of education (Wenger, 1998: 263–277).

Making Communities of Practice work in formal education

The challenge, therefore, is to take a series of ideas that were originally brought together in order to provide a new explanatory framework for apprenticeship learning in everyday workplace settings, and rework them in such a way that we can use them to design new practices within formal educational settings, in a similar manner to the way in which other researchers and writers have already reworked them in order to explore existing practices in not only further and adult education (as seen in the examples discussed in Chapter 3) but in schools, universities, and organisational learning. But this time, our reworking is based on ideas set out by one of the original authors of CoP theory rather than ideas that have been added to the CoP field later on. The surprising thing (for me, anyway) is that these ideas for reworking have not been more widely used.

In the last section of the *Communities of Practice* book, titled 'Epilogue: Design', Wenger sets out for the first time a clear statement as to how the insights generated through the broader discussion of social learning within Communities of Practice might be applied to formal educational contexts (1998: 223–278), challenging head-on the refutations of formal pedagogy and schooling found within the earlier book (Lave and Wenger, 1991: 99–100, 107–108). In order to do this, Wenger takes three theoretical steps – although these should be considered as overlapping rather than as arranged in a hierarchical order. First, he explains how the ideas of 'teaching' and 'curriculum' might be inserted into the detailed framework for CoPs that he has already laid out in his book. Next, he draws on the social theory of learning that he has explored, and that moves us away from just the newcomers and apprentices learning through LPP. And thirdly, he describes a theoretical framework for designing for learning that includes all of the key components of his work – a framework that he calls a **Learning Architecture**.

A Learning Architecture is a framework for designing learning. More specifically, it is a framework for designing social and physical spaces where opportunities for learning are made available to all of those people who are within that space. It is impossible to build a Community of Practice from scratch because that's not how they work. What you *can* do is build a Learning Architecture, which in turn will allow a Community of Practice to emerge. But there is no point in trying to establish a Learning Architecture that will help generate CoPs in a further education college, for example, unless there is a way of explaining how a CoP can actually work within a college – or any other educational institution for that matter – in the first place. When we go into detail about what needs to be included within a Learning Architecture (I shall return to this shortly) we are working towards establishing that CoP whilst also acknowledging that things might turn out a little differently.

One way to think about this is to consider an example from *curriculum theory*, which is (or ought to be) a key curriculum component for all Cert Ed and PGCE programmes in the post-compulsory sector (Curzon and Tummons, 2013; Tummons, 2012). Curriculum theory provides a number of conceptual tools to help us think about the courses and programmes of study that we teach, interpret, and sometimes design. These tools are often presented as two-part models, where each part is different from the other but both are needed in order to make sense of the ideas at work. These (borrowing a bit of jargon from philosophy) are referred to as *dualisms*. So, for example, one dualism that we find in curriculum theory is *curriculum as product* versus *curriculum as process*. This is the idea that any evaluation of a curriculum tends to focus either on the end result for the student who has successfully gone through the curriculum – the product – or on the experiences of the student during their time within the curriculum – the process. These are usually dependent on the theory of learning (again, as found in Cert Ed and PGCE courses) that underpins the curriculum: behaviourist or neo-behaviourist theories inform a product approach, while constructivist theories inform a process approach.

Another dualism is curriculum as *planned* or *specified* versus curriculum as *received* or *enacted* (both sets of labels can be found in the literature but they mean broadly the same thing). This dualism allows us to think about the differences between how a course or programme of study might look on the pages of an awarding body specification, compared to how it really happens in the classroom. For example: it is easy to imagine that a tutor or trainer might do things differently from one year to the next, not because the unit of study has been changed, but because the trainees are different from one year to the next and might respond better to different choices of activity or resource, for example. Or we might imagine a single group of students responding to the arrival of a replacement tutor at a midway point in the academic year. The module that they are studying has stayed the same, the materials and content are the same, but the teaching style will be different and that will have an impact on how the module feels for the students and how they respond to it. The concept of curriculum as planned versus curriculum as received makes us acknowledge that any programme of study will always be a little bit different, depending on who teaches it, who the students are and where they come from, what resources are available, what the teaching accommodation is like, and so forth. When quality assurance processes talk about standardisation, what they are actually doing is making things 'standardised enough' to prevent too many different practices from generating an unfair or unbalanced curriculum across the sector as a whole.

A curriculum can never turn out exactly as planned. Neither can a Community of Practice that has been set in motion by the establishment of a Learning Architecture. And this is for the simple reason that learning – according to the social theory of learning – is always a little unpredictable, always changing shape, happening a bit differently to how we might think. It is categorically *not* messy (a term that gets waved around by some theorists and writers, often incorrectly). But it is *emergent*: that is to say, it is a process and not a product, and a process that is always – even if only very gradually – changing and adapting. The **practice** of the community provides the space and time for learning to happen, and the learning provides a structure for the practice, enriches it and even helps to change it (Wenger, 1998: 96–98). Or, to put it another way, learning and practice are a dualism – each working with and alongside the other. Learning isn't something that just gets switched on and off when you arrive and then leave college: it happens all of the time. The way that we learn at college is no different to the way that we learn outside college. It is the structures, tools, routines, people, and resources that vary. Those structures, tools, routines, people, and resources that might be found within any Community of Practice often come together in informal, non-linear ways, gathered together over time – and that is very much the idea of the CoP suggested by Lave and Wenger (1991). But the structures and so forth might also be brought together deliberately, as part of a conscious effort to encourage a specified body of learning to emerge, collected together within a Learning Architecture. The CoP cannot be predicted or specified, reduced to a list: nor can the learning that might happen within and around it. You cannot design a CoP, and you cannot design learning. But you can design *for* learning, using a Learning Architecture.

With all of this in mind, we can go back to the three steps that Wenger takes in order to translate CoPs from being focussed on apprentices, outside institutions and in opposition to pedagogy and formal educational curricula, to being a tool for exploring the practices of learning within a further education college or adult education centre. I should also add here that although the framework presented is derived entirely from Wenger (1998), dividing it into these three steps is my way of breaking things down into small components (and Wenger's original discussion is more elegantly expressed than I can hope to manage) as there are a lot of ideas to get used to, and they are not intended as a list where one follows the other. Rather, these three steps all need to be taken at the same time.

First step: how can we include pedagogy, teaching, and curriculum within a CoP?

Teaching is a complex social process that nonetheless is only one element of what goes on in a workshop or college: without the necessary, authentic, resources for a course or module, teaching cannot work in the way that it needs to or is intended. Once again, curriculum theory helps us here, and specifically the concept of the *total curriculum* – the idea that for any curriculum to be properly understood we need to consider absolutely everything that the curriculum needs in order to be accomplished – teachers, materials, rooms, documents, tools, and so forth (Kelly, 2009). Or, as Wenger puts it, 'learning is an emergent, ongoing process, which may use teaching as *one of its many structuring resources*' (1998: 267, emphasis added). From this perspective, teaching can here be understood as being one component of a Learning Architecture, rather than a separate process that stands outside it. Teaching becomes part of the

shared repertoire of the Community of Practice. Therefore, just like the other parts of the shared repertoire of *any* CoP, it – that is to say, the practice of teaching, of pedagogy – is a cultural tool that can be employed by those members of the community who have the appropriate expertise to use it: the teachers. The same holds true for assessment and feedback, which we shall return to in Chapter 7.

Second step: what does a social theory of learning imply for teaching and learning within a formal educational setting?

College lecturers and assessors are all-too familiar with various models of lesson observation (OTL – 'observing teaching and learning'), sometimes conducted for the purposes of evaluation, sometimes for developmental reasons, and sometimes for a combination of the two. Over time, 'on-the-spot' graded lesson observations have given way to more developmental approaches. But what do OTLs actually do? Research from the Education Endowment Foundation suggests that their impact is minimal in terms of improved outcomes for students (Worth et al., 2017). And the extent to which any kind of observation is valid or reliable is also questionable, not least because learning is invisible and so we rely on proxies instead, such as seeing a 'busy' environment or observing that students are 'interested' (Coe et al., 2014). CoP theory raises a more fundamental concern, however. Remembering the social theory of learning on the one hand, and the practice of teaching on the other, Wenger concludes that '*teaching does not cause learning*: what ends up being taught may or may not be what was taught, or more generally what the institutional organisation of instruction intended' (1998: 267, emphasis added). That is to say, teaching no more directly causes learning to happen than does the provision of a set of tools, or a series of instructional manuals. Nor can we isolate the teaching from the other elements of the architecture – it is an integral part of the CoP, just as learning is. If we recall that teaching is just one of several structuring resources within a CoP, then the emphasis shifts from the teacher to the apprentice or student, who will have to do the effortful work of learning within the CoP in order to travel along their chosen and/or required **trajectories** (as discussed in Chapter 2). Learning is another form of practice: it takes work and requires active engagement by the apprentice with all of the structuring resources at their disposal – including, but by no means restricted to, teaching.

Third step: what are the different parts of a Learning Architecture?

A full explanation of why Learning Architectures work in the way that they do requires a discussion of those aspects of CoP theory that underpin them, and I shall return to this shortly. For now, it is sufficient to note the more practical and everyday components of a Learning Architecture – which in fact will be entirely familiar to many, if not all, of the readers of this book. For convenience, we might at first split them into three categories – although they all overlap in practice. First, we have material or physical resources: workshop tools, stools and chairs, data projectors and tablet PCs, graph paper, pencils, books, PDF files, and so forth. In a way, we can include people in this category as well, and this might include trainers and teachers, but also visitors, perhaps employers (for students on T-level placement, for example), internal moderators and external verifiers, even admissions tutors (who need to let you in to the CoP in the first place). Second, we have immaterial or non-physical resources: routines, attitudes, feelings. For example, a student working towards a level 3 CACHE Award in Childcare and Education will need to develop and embody an *ethic* of care and professionalism or an understanding of a child's *right* to play as much as a theoretical understanding of those same things. Third, we have processes and procedures: teaching, assessment, demonstrations, moderation meetings, placements, admissions, tutorials, validation events, and so forth – any kind of habitual, routinised form of activity, which will both require and allow the use of different kinds of material or physical resources, and different kinds of non-physical resources as well.

Interlude: why are there not more articles and books about Learning Architectures?

In comparison to other elements of Wenger's book, it can be unambiguously argued that the Learning Architecture is under-explored, and I for one am at a loss to explain why this might be. The way in which different theories get used – or not – seems somewhat arbitrary, and certainly not straightforwardly connected to the value, rigour, or appropriateness of the theory in question. If only the 'good' theories made it into our professional qualifications, experiences and lives, we would never have heard of learning styles or thinking hats!

A small number of articles have drawn on Learning Architectures. Brosnan and Burgess (2003) applied the framework to an exploration of online continuing professional development courses for health and social care staff. Sorensen and Ó Murchú (2004) explored online modules for Masters-degree students. And McCloughlin and colleagues (2008) drew on Learning Architectures in designing programmes for pre-service secondary teachers. Smith (2009) reported on an ethnographic study of one young child over an 18-month period in order to explore the Learning Architectures that shaped her progress through childcare and into primary education. Scanlan's (2012) similarly immersive research involved a year-long study of educational leadership as a tool for promoting social justice through education. There's nothing yet that is directly linked to the further and adult education sector (and this is not much of a surprise) but the works cited here are worth following up for anyone with a theoretical interest.

The conceptual foundations of a Learning Architecture

By now, we have a good understanding of a **social theory of learning**, of how learning, and a particular form of learning for newcomers or apprentices

(**Legitimate Peripheral Participation**) is to be found within **Communities of Practice**, and how – if we want to design an environment for some planned or intended learning to happen – we can assemble a **Learning Architecture**. The final stage in this part of our account is, therefore, to consider the theoretical underpinnings of the Learning Architecture, of which there are four different parts. Each part pulls together different elements of CoP theory more generally, some of which we have already discussed, and others which will be new to us. Some of these new elements will be explored in detail, and we shall return to a small number of others in more depth in later chapters. Once again, we have some new terminology to get used to. The four parts of a Learning Architecture are:

1 Reification and participation.
2 Designed and emergent.
3 Local and global.
4 Identification and negotiability.

And we shall go through each one in turn, remembering once again that these are always inter-related and work equally to support a Learning Architecture – one element is not more important than any other.

Reification and participation

The social theory of learning rests on the core assumption that learning involves the whole person. It is not simply a cognitive process, but a process involving knowing in doing things, talking with people, trying things out, and both seeing how things work or are done and being allowed to do those same things. When new members join in order to learn the practices of a community, they need to be given opportunities to take part in the authentic practice of the community: to participate. As we have already seen, participation will be peripheral at first and then will become more full over time. The participation of the new arrivals is not only characterised by **participation** – by doing things, but also by making things, by having a concrete impact on the practices at hand, even if only peripherally – and this is referred to as **reification** (Wenger, 1998). To reify something means to turn something that is abstract into a physical or concrete thing. For example, a group of tutors might all attend the same standardisation meeting and the minutes of the meeting, which recorded what standardisation processes were done and why, would be an example of a reification. Our group of CACHE level 3 students will, by the end of their course, know lots of things about how best to *support emergent literacy* in an early years setting, and the resources that they create – and then include in their portfolios – are likewise examples of reifications. Reification and participation always go together: practice (which always involves learning) leads to the creation of things, objects, and all kinds of other stuff that encapsulate, make visible, allow, help, and make (more-or-less) permanent the practices being done within that the community: participation always involves reification (this is discussed further in Chapter 7).

The reification/participation dualism focuses attention, therefore, on the balance that has to be established to allow apprentices or newcomers firstly to come to know about, use, or otherwise draw on the existing tools, objects, and artefacts of a community, and secondly to amend, add to, edit, or reconfigure these same tools and objects, and to use them to create, shape, or alter other things as well. It is through a process of **negotiation** (Wenger, 1998: 264) between both participation and reification that people are able to learn. If the trainee is provided with opportunities for participation that do not include reification, then learning is impaired – it becomes **illegitimate** because without reification, it cannot be authentic. A trainee bicycle mechanic cannot learn very much if she is only allowed to watch what happens in the workshop: she needs to be allowed to pick up and then use different tools, to learn their names ('fourth hand tool', 'crank extractor') and when best to use each one, and in turn to establish her own work routines or procedures (which job to do first, how best to note down the spare parts that needed to be replaced). Trainee hairdressers do not attempt, nor would they be allowed to attempt, complicated hair styling during their first few days at work in a salon. Instead, they perform smaller jobs and less critical tasks that are nonetheless authentic because they still involve both participation (such as helping to fetch equipment for shampooing a client's hair or learning how to use the booking system) and reification (knowing what the equipment does and learning how to manipulate it, or generating a new diary entry for a client appointment).

Designed and emergent

A social model of learning tells us that learning in a CoP is a fluid, complex, and possibly also troublesome phenomenon. It cannot be predicted or straightforwardly itemised on a checklist. It is possible to specify some of the background conditions that are required for learning to happen (access to authentic practice, acceptance by and guidance from acknowledged expert practitioners, availability of appropriate materials and tools, and so forth), but it is not possible to specify *exactly* what will be learned – only that learning will be taking place, as a consequence of participation. Consequently, the design of a Learning Architecture has to be mindful of the different ways in which students will go about the 'work' of learning: learning requires effort and application, irrespective of what it is that is being learned. This work will include how the newcomers talk about and work with the resources provided, the ways in which different teachers interact with their students (remember – it's work for us as well), the ways in which the tools or materials work, and so on. Things such as these all make a difference to how learning happens – that is, to the lived experience of participation (or LPP for the newcomers specifically) within the CoP.

When designing a learning architecture we can anticipate, to a high degree of appropriateness and accuracy (derived from our own knowing, our own occupational and professional histories or trajectories, and the expertise and experience gathered during our own time served within either this or related CoPs), the stuff that we, as teachers and trainers, might need. This includes the reifications that we create for use with our students (handouts or PowerPoints, activities, formative, and/or practice tasks) as well as the reifications that come from outside our immediate community, but which can be brought across **boundaries** into our own (new workshop or laboratory equipment that we might need training in how to use before term starts, books purchased for the library, websites that are subscribed to). All of these elements are part of the design for the Learning Architecture, and these are elements that *can* be listed, audited, and even put on a checklist. But these elements cannot be straight-forwardly or unproblematically evaluated. We can never know exactly how different students will react to our choice of activities, our experiments or our lectures, from one year to the next. Each student is an individual, enfolded within an individual biography and history that impacts on their learning as they travel along their unique trajectory within the CoP. Consequently the nature of their participation is similarly unique, although it may well be the case that the trajectories of a cohort of students, considered as a group, and the natures of their respective participations are very closely aligned and are very similar in lots of ways. But it is not the case that just because students partici-pate, they do so in ways *exactly* determined by staff. We have established that learning is an emergent process and teaching is just one of the **structuring resources** that newcomers might use. But what matters here is not a focus on how teaching impacts on learning – because it is hard, if not impossible, to directly link the two – but rather, how teaching and learning can 'interact so as to become structuring resources for each other' (Wenger, 1998: 267). A focus on Learning Architecture allows us to focus on the relationship between teaching, which is **designed**, and learning, which is **emergent**. Practice – and, therefore, learning – is not the *result* of design, but an emergent *response* to it.

Local and global

At this point, we can be confident in saying that Communities of Practice do not exist in isolation: earlier references to **boundaries** and **constellations** have hinted at the more extensive discussion of relationships between CoPs that we will turn to in Chapter 6. For the present, it is sufficient to understand that arrangements of CoPs – sometimes quite alike, sometimes very different – exist in such a way as to allow for the movement of both people and things (tools, habits, texts, machines) between them. No CoP, therefore, exists in isolation. Nor is any CoP entirely homegrown, indigenous in its culture. Any account of a CoP, therefore, will need in some way to at least acknowledge the ways in which the practices of that community are shared with or borrowed from another. This will of course vary according to the nature, proximity, and intensity of the relationships between them. Sometimes, a CoP will have a close relationship with a neighbour or set of neighbours, allowing members and materials to cross the boundaries between them in a straightforward manner. At other times, however, **boundary crossing** might be restricted or even discouraged. The links from one community to another can be plentiful and obvious, or minimal and difficult to identify, but they are always present. Traces of these links might be found in how community members talk, particular activities that the community might encourage or discourage, how tools and artefacts have been built or used, and so forth. Simply put, we can say that every Community of Practice consists of elements that are both **local** (that is to say, native or indigenous) and **global** (that is, borrowed, donated, stolen or shared from elsewhere within the wider constellation).

The balance between the global and the local can be mapped out in all kinds of ways. Some of these balances have to be considered in terms of the balance of influence or power between communities – for example, in the ways in which particular curricula are required to map onto an externally prescribed series of occupational standards so that a specific endorsement or process of accreditation overseen by a relevant trade or professional body might be made available to students on successful completion of the programme. For example, the *Association of Accounting Technicians* (AAT) has supported the development of three levels of *Apprenticeship Standards*; the *Hair and Beauty Industry Authority* (Habia) similarly supported the development of National Occupational Standards (NOS). Or we might consider the role performed by an external verifier, who can provide insights from the wider landscape of practices, across the further education and skills sector as a whole, that might be applied at local college level. Other traces of the global in the local are more small-scale, such as the way in which a website can provide a window into a wider constellation of practices than might otherwise be practicable, or the ways in which a group activity can be enriched through the contributions of visiting members of a profession or trade. Thus, the relationship between the global and the local is accomplished through the movement of both people and things across different kinds of geographical, institutional, and even temporal boundaries. It might not always be necessary to trace those networks through which the global impacts on the local, or along which the local reports back to the global, but if they are to form a focus for inquiry, then we need to be mindful of how they are constituted in terms of the relationships between the people and the stuff who make up the constellation. How far and how fast they can travel, how successfully they travel, or what happens at the end of the journey, may all need to be accounted for.

Identification and negotiability

Membership, and therefore learning, within a community of practice always involves **identity**. When a newcomer engages in practice through legitimate peripheral participation – in the enterprise of the community, working with or creating reifications, learning the talk or discourse of the community – she begins to reconstruct her identity. At the same time the CoP adjusts around her, and the other members come to know who she is and to acknowledge her identity as a peripheral member at first and a full member over time. Sometimes, identity is easy to spot and will be accomplished through a process of recognition involving things rather than people: the wearing of a uniform (commonly found amongst Entry to Uniformed Services students, for example), or the wearing of an identity or library card in a lanyard around the neck (more common). At other times, identity can be observed through actions (the mastery of a complex manual task) and speech (using key terminology or jargon during a conversation).

Identity needs to be understood in terms of both person and context. It is a product of a two-way process between the CoP member – her prior history, her experiences, her wearing of a lanyard, her decision whether to carry her portfolio under her arm or inside a satchel – and her environment – the college or work-place as a whole, the particular places within them that she occupies, the people she talks to and works with. This two-way process is referred to as **negotiation**, the capacity to 'shape the meanings that matter within a social configuration' (Wenger, 1998: 197). That is to say, it is through being able to contribute to the actions, discussions, or reifications of the CoP in a meaningful way that participation is not only engaged but also deepened. Such meaning making always relies on the trajectory and position of the participant, however: a newcomer often cannot modify or control the meanings that are being negotiated to the same degree as an old-timer. Nonetheless, negotiation is always present.

If a community of practice is going to thrive (which is by no means guaranteed – communities always have to work to sustain themselves), it needs to allow all of the members to reconcile the need to match up to the requirements or standards of the community on the one hand, with the ability and opportunity to act independently within it on the other. If our student feels powerless or ignored within any particular CoP, then she will become alienated from it and consequently will not feel able or willing to participate and as a result will not be able to learn. If, however, learners are able to make some kind of choice or informed input regarding aspects of their practice, then their participation, and hence their learning, will be deeper and more meaningful. Therefore, a balance needs to be struck regarding the extent to which members **identify** with the practices, goals, or aspirations of a community, and the extent to which members can **negotiate** aspects of their practice. The CoP needs this balance between identity and negotiation in order to function, and it involves all of the members of the community (newcomers and old-timers) engaging in two different – but complementary – modes of work (Wenger, 1998: 220): **identification work**, and **participation work**. Identification work describes those ways in which people work to help others feel part of a community, as well as establishing themselves as members, and requires things from individual members such as acceptance of habits and rules, making a commitment to the community, and such like. Participation work describes those ways in which members not only engage in the practice of the community but also build their relationships with other members, and requires things such as listening to other perspectives, sharing resources, coming to a consensus, managing confrontation, compromise, and so forth.

Putting it all together: Learning Architectures, further education, and skills

Course and programme design is a commonplace task for many teachers and trainers in further and adult education. Most of us will spend much of our time working with a curriculum scheme that has been provided by an awarding body that leaves little room for flexibility or customisation: our job is to interpret and then 'deliver' the curriculum that we are responsible for. Some of us will be required to draw up much more detailed schema, perhaps even to design entire modules and programmes for the purposes of validation. And sometimes our work will involve a bit of both. For anyone with responsibilities for designing and/or implementing a curriculum – and here I include not only teachers and trainers but also members of those external bodies that draw up National Occupational Standards, employers, and so forth – there are three needs that must be met if students are going to be able to participate and, therefore, learn. These are elegantly summarised by Wenger (1998: 271) and are worth quoting in full:

1. Places of engagement.
2. Materials and experiences with which to build an image of the world and themselves.
3. Ways of having an effect on the world and making their actions matter.

None of these needs are, in and of themselves, novel or unexpected. Even the newest FE college teacher, freshly enrolled on a part-time Cert Ed programme, is aware of the importance of appropriate teaching accommodation, fitted out with the right equipment and resources so that the students are able to experience an authentic sample of what the 'real world' of the occupation or trade that they are learning will feel like. The notion that a greater familiarity with the tools of the trade will help apprentices build confidence as well as competence is similarly unsurprising. And there can be few trainees who would happily agree to performing tasks or practicing techniques that did not in some way align to the real world of work – or further study – that they imagine for themselves. Or, to put it another way, just as Communities of Practice are already present in workplaces, colleges, and adult education centres (as we discussed in Chapter 1), so many aspects of Learning Architectures are also already there. Our job is to identify what's there so that we can plug any gaps, and use CoP theory to explain how and why the Learning Architecture will work in the way that it does. In this way we can answer the question 'what use is theory?' by answering that 'theory provides robust ways for explaining the things that are around us.'

In summing up, we can therefore state that:

1   A Learning Architecture is nothing more than the entire infrastructure – of people, resources, places – that a Community of Practice requires. This may include rooms, workbenches, assessments, websites, technicians, teachers, books, tools, portfolios, guest speakers, placements – anything, in fact, that is needed.

2   Any deficit in the authenticity of the Learning Architecture will always, necessarily, impact on the authenticity of the learning that will emerge. (Many years ago, I was visiting a land-based college in order to do Cert Ed/PGCE observations. I was observing an animal management class – *Looking After Exotic Animals.* At the college, they had no exotic animals for the students to work with.)

3   A Community of Practice cannot be specified in advance or predicted, but a Learning Architecture can be.

4   A CoP is never isolated: it is always in connection with, and overlapping with, other CoPs. As such, elements of the Learning Architecture – and therefore the CoP in turn – will always come from outside. This may include more obvious elements such as programme handbooks (from awarding bodies) and occupational standards (from professional bodies), as well as the people who might accompany such elements – moderators and verifiers, workplace trainers, or placement coordinators. Elements such as tools and equipment (which reflect the history of the practice or occupation more broadly) will also travel from the global context of the curriculum/ occupation to the local context of the workshop or classroom.

5   Once the CoP is established, it is not possible to predict exactly what learning will happen, when, and in what order. It is possible to establish a broadly generalisable account of the learning that will take place, but there will always be unanticipated variation due to the emergent nature of learning.

6   The emergent nature of learning within a CoP means that there is no 'right' way through which learning might happen. At the same time, there is no direct link between teaching and learning: learning relies equally on all of the resources of the Learning Architecture, not just one of them. This has important consequences for quality assurance and especially for the practice of lesson observation: observations should encompass all elements of the Learning Architecture equally and not only, or mainly, the teaching.

Some conclusions

As originally constructed, the theory of **situated learning** within a Community of Practice was deliberately placed outside formal educational contexts. As we have seen in this chapter, it is through the careful application of the later theoretical innovations of Wenger (1998) that we can instead translate CoPs into colleges and adult education centres. I am deliberately excluding workplaces for now, because, as places, they tend to be characterised by already-existing CoPs rather than newly emergent CoPs that have been established purely for the purposes of accomplishing the delivery of a formal programme of study. Nonetheless, as we shall see in more detail in Chapter 6, workplaces are enrolled within the constellations of CoPs that also include formal educational establishments. For now, it is sufficient to note that within formal education and training, the specification of a Learning Architecture is the first step in allowing a CoP to emerge. Within that – and every other – CoP, learning remains emergent and unpredictable, and certainly not reliant only on teaching as a structuring resource. It is not possible to separate teaching from the other elements of the community, if we are trying to make sense of or even evaluate the practice of teaching (and I would argue that to try to evaluate teaching in isolation is a mistake). Instead, we need to contextualise teaching within the broader practices of the communities within which we practice.

References

Brosnan, K. and Burgess, R. (2003) Web based continuing professional development – a learning architecture approach. *Journal of Workplace Learning* 15 (1) 24–33. doi:10.1108/13665620310458794.

Coe, R., Aloisi, C., Higgins, S., and Elliot Major, L. (2014) *What makes great teaching?* London: The Sutton Trust.

Curzon, L. B. and Tummons, J. (2013) *Teaching in Further Education: an outline of principles and practice.* Seventh edition. London: Bloomsbury.

Kelly, A. V. (2009) *The Curriculum: theory and practice.* Sixth edition. London: Sage.

Lave, J. and Wenger, E. (1991) *Situated Learning: Legitimate Peripheral Participation.* Cambridge: Cambridge University Press.

McLoughlin, M., Lee, M. and Brady, J. (2008) A learning architecture framework (LAF) for developing community, engagement and professional identity for pre-service teachers. In Olney, I., Lefoe, G., Mantei, J. and Herrington, J. (eds.) *Proceedings of the Second Emerging Technologies Conference 2008.* Wollongong: University of Wollongong. 147–157.

Scanlan, M. (2012) A learning architecture: how school leaders can design for learning social justice. *Educational Administration Quarterly* 49 (2) 348–391. doi:10.1177%2F0013161X12456699.

Smith, A. (2009) A case study of learning architecture and reciprocity. *International Journal of Early Childhood* 41 (1) 33–49.

Sorensen, E. and Ó Murchú, D. (2004) Designing online learning communities of practice: a democratic perspective. *Journal of Educational Media* 29 (3) 189–200. doi:10.1080/1358165042000283066.

Tummons, J. (2012) *Curriculum Studies in the Lifelong Learning Sector.* Second edition. London: Sage/Learning Matters.

Tummons, J. (2018) *Learning architectures in higher education: beyond communities of practice.* London: Bloomsbury.

Wenger, E. (1998) *Communities of Practice: Learning, Meaning and Identity.* Cambridge: Cambridge University Press.

Worth, J., Sizmur, J., Walker, M., Bradshaw, S., and Styles, B. (2017) *Teacher Observation.* London: Education Endowment Foundation.

5 What can Communities of Practice actually do? And what can't they do?

Introduction

In this fifth chapter, I am going to pull on the work of a number of different researchers who over time have explored a range of topics that will be immediately familiar to new as well as experienced practitioners in further and adult education. These issues include the ways in which some courses have predominantly female cohorts whilst others have mostly male cohorts, the provision of level 1 courses for so-called 'at risk' learners, subsequent changes to professional standards for teachers and trainers in the sector, and the use of Individual Learning Plans. In the process, I will outline ways in which we can explore things that CoP theory is not so well suited for. In doing so, I do not seek to build new theoretical models, but instead simply to show how other research can sit alongside the work of Lave and Wenger, and Wenger, acknowledging the limits of CoP theory in a constructive manner.

The story so far

By this stage of the journey, some of you will have realised that I take theory use seriously. This is not, however, a consequence of some form of academic snobbery or elitism: it is simply the case that I want educational researchers to use theory with the exact same care and diligence that a skilled, careful teacher of apprentice car mechanics uses specialist pieces of equipment pulled from a tool board to demonstrate a new technique to a group of learners, or a reflective, experienced English to Speakers of Other Languages (ESOL) teacher uses carefully designed and/or selected resources in their classroom. We wouldn't rely on a mechanic who cannot use their tools properly; nor should we rely on researchers that cannot use theory properly. Yes, there is room for sometimes considerable debate and discussion, but theory, like a piece of resistant metal, can only be bent out of shape so far before it becomes denatured. So, when I see something described as a Community of Practice, my first response is to ask: on what basis have you applied your description? Does your account demonstrate that you have thought and read carefully about CoPs, and have applied the label thoughtfully, and not just from a well-meant but under-theorised standpoint?

DOI: 10.4324/9781003252566-5

These are important questions because of the claims that are sometimes made for the benefits (possible disadvantages rarely get mentioned, as we shall see) of Communities of Practice. A CoP has been established, or a list of CoPs has been collected and evaluated, we are told, and membership of one or more of these will have a number of benefits for our professional practice. They will lead to collaboration and quality improvement. They will lead to the sharing of digital pedagogical skills. They can even save on costs and improve efficiency. But there are two kinds of problem that stem from this approach. First, there is the simple fact that such theory-light approaches lack rigour or depth. We established in Chapter 1 that careful and critical use of theory is necessary if we are going to use that theory in a predictive manner. We cannot take seriously any kind of theory-based predictive modelling if the theory in question has only been very briefly sketched. And second, there is the 'behavioural objectives' style in which such claims inevitably get reduced to: 'by the end of your engagement with this Community of Practice you will have shared best practice, gained professional knowledge, and improved efficiency.' Statements such as these are, simply put, illogical and perhaps even nonsensical. If you subscribe to a CoP-informed perspective, then you will know (thanks to careful and thorough reading) that learning cannot be predicted in such a manner. Learning within any and every CoP is always emergent and unpredictable (as we have seen in Chapter 2) and cannot be specified in advance. And yet it is not too difficult to find inflated and/or uncritical claims for the benefits of CoPs such as these. If, therefore, we are to construct a more serious and well-thought answer to the question 'what can CoPs do?' we should probably also answer the obvious next question, 'what can CoPs *not* do?'

Hopefully, it will not take too long to discuss what CoPs *can* do: after all, much of our discussion thus far has been centred on the value and utility of a CoP-led perspective for the further and adult education sector. Up to this point, our line of analysis is as follows:

1　A Community of Practice is a shared space – physical and/or online – in which people have grouped together in order to take part in a shared form of practice.
2　Practices are many and varied – some are time-consuming and complex, and others are more straightforward. Some involve complicated equipment, esoteric bodies of knowledge, and specialist ways of talking and/or writing.
3　Participation is also varied: some people will travel towards the centre of the community whilst others will always only stay nearer the boundaries; some will change their direction of travel, and others will leave after a short time.
4　Any CoP always involves learning, which is understood as a social practice. Learning is a necessary consequence of participation within the community.
5　Particular opportunities for new members of the community always need to be made available if they are going to be able to take part and hence to learn – this learning is described as Legitimate Peripheral Participation.

6   Communities of Practice are everywhere and evolve over time. They always change – sometimes quickly and sometimes slowly. Sometimes they fade away. At others times they change quite radically.

7   Communities of Practice never exist in isolation: they are always part of a wider constellation of CoPs, sometimes close together and sometimes at a distance. Borders overlap, people visit other CoPs and can be members of many, and objects, routines, ways of talking, and artefacts from one CoP can be borrowed – or stolen – by another.

8   A Community of Practice cannot be designed in a top-down manner and then opened up for membership. Instead, we can design a Learning Architecture from which a CoP will develop. This allows us to place CoPs within formal educational structures/contexts.

9   Learning (according to our social theory) is emergent – it doesn't travel in a straight line. Therefore the nature of CoPs is also emergent.

10   There are many social configurations of people and things that are of great interest to us as education researchers, but are not automatically CoPs. If we want to know if something is a CoP or not, then we have to do some (almost certainly ethnographic) research.

What can a Community of Practice do, therefore? It can be a shared space for learning, allowing anyone who joins that space to learn more about practice through an authentic engagement with it. It can bring together the full range of materials, people, routines, words, and habits that make up any specialist craft, occupation, body of knowledge or profession, and make them available for both the apprentice or beginner who is just starting out and the experienced old-timer who still wishes to learn. It can be a place where the newcomer can learn from conversations with peers and advice from more experienced neighbours, or where a longer-standing member of the community can pick up new techniques that the newcomer has brought with them from a different community. Practitioners can beg, borrow, and steal from neighbouring CoPs, allowing ideas, tools, people, expertise, and workarounds to be shared across **boundaries**, and can send out their own in turn. They can be engaging, innovative, welcoming, and nurturing. And they can also be none of those things.

What Can't Communities of Practice Do?

One of the criticisms that has, not without some justification, been levelled at the broader CoP literature is that it tends to always position CoPs as being benign and friendly places, with disagreements restricted to polite conversations about the technical or professional matters at hand. Yes, there are possibilities for conflict – but these are framed in terms of an inter-generational conflict of practices or ideas, where the conflict is between practices, habits, and repertoires, not between people. Some of the more critical voices in the literature argue that CoP theory lacks a way of accounting for conflict, for inequalities of power, for dealing with diversity and stigma. Others have suggested that CoP theory cannot accommodate wider societal issues, or account for the broader social and historical contexts in which CoPs find themselves. They look outward to other CoPs and other constellations, but they do not look at the rest of the world. For some writers, many of these concerns are due to flaws in CoP theory itself, generated as a result of incomplete or vague theorising, or even due to a failure to consider certain key issues in the first place, and they have resolved these deficiencies through using other theoretical frameworks, plugging them in to CoPs (as discussed in Chapter 3). But if we move beyond the theoretical and start to consider more pragmatic issues, we can build a clearer picture of the limits of CoP theory. By this, I mean to stress that there is clearly a difference between resolving a theoretical deficiency within CoP theory in response to a perceived problem, and a recognition of a limitation in CoP theory that, if acknowledged, does not stop us from using CoP theory but simply causes us to do so cautiously, avoiding overblown or unrealistic claims.

Let me provide an example: one of the plug-ins for CoP theory that I discussed in Chapter 3 pertained to gender, drawing on the work of Paechter (2003), who proposed constructing masculinities and femininities as Communities of Practice, employing Wenger's (1998) conceptions of **boundary** and **identity** in doing so. Now, this discussion raises all kinds of interesting and important topics for discussion about how gender identity is acquired or learned at a social level. But it doesn't really help us to explore how somebody's gender might impact on their identity formation or their **trajectory** within another CoP such as might be found in a stereotypically 'male' subject area such as *light vehicle mechanical maintenance* or, conversely, a stereotypically 'female' subject area such as *hair and media make-up*. The idea that some subject areas can be gendered is well-established within education research, although, as usual, the number of papers and chapters that explore this issue in an FE setting is dwarfed by the number of papers that discuss schools or universities. But CoP theory, in and of itself, does not have any tools with which to tackle this issue (Hughes et al., 2007).

Interlude: the gendered nature of further education colleges

Our current discussion provides a good opportunity to introduce the *Transforming Learning Cultures in Further Education* project, although some of the readers of this book will have come across it before. This project, the first ever large-scale and independent study of learning and teaching in the English further education sector, ran from 2001 to 2005, and the book that encapsulated the project as a whole, *Improving Learning Cultures in Further Education* was published two years later (James and Biesta, 2007). One of the earlier publications that came out of the project, written by Helen Colley and colleagues, explored the experiences of students as they followed particular programmes of study and adapted to the cultures of the particular subject areas that they chose (Colley et al., 2003). Interestingly, and mindful of the arguments that I am making in this book, Colley et al. rejected an approach to their research based on Lave and Wenger (1991) on the grounds that Lave and Wenger's 'exclusive emphasis on the authenticity of workplace learning means that they tend to dismiss the value of learning in more formal educational settings such as FE' (2003: 475).

In the paper, a number of different level 3 courses were explored: childcare, health studies, and electronic engineering, each at a different college. The first two of these were full-time college courses, punctuated with work placements; the third organised on a day-release basis. One of the findings from the data discussed in this paper (the data set for the project as a whole was considerably larger) related to gender and specifically to the ways in which the different curricula carried different gendered identities. In the childcare course, all of the students were female and aged 16–17 except for one mature female and one male, studying in an 'overwhelmingly female' department (Colley et al., 2003: 480). In health studies, all of the students were female, again working within a 'strongly gendered physical location within the college', in which one of the students 'described the engineering department – populated predominantly by male mechanics and welding students – as "the scary places" in the college, and as "non-girl territory"' (2003., 483). In engineering, by contrast, all of the students bar one were male.

A discussion of gender such as this falls outside the remit of CoP theory: gender, as a sociological or conceptual factor, simply does not figure in Wenger's account; nor does it figure in the earlier work with Lave. Gender, therefore, can be described as belonging to our first category of things that CoPs cannot do: it is *absent* from CoP theory.

Absences: areas of research interest that are absent from CoP theory

Arguably, any theory is necessarily incomplete. The only thing that comes close to a theory of everything is in theoretical physics of the kind done by Albert Einstein and Stephen Hawking. For education researchers, and social scientists more generally, our theoretical frameworks are more modest and incapable of covering everything. As such, when we say that CoP theory doesn't have an element within it that allow us to focus on gender, we are critiquing CoP theory but we are not criticising it. The distinction between these two is important. When we criticise, we disapprove of and dismiss something on the grounds that we have perceived a fault to be within it. When we critique, we provide a detailed analysis and evaluation of something. A critique of CoP theory on the basis that it lacks a way of accounting for gender does not automatically imply a dismissal or rejection of CoP theory. Instead, it simply means that we are using CoP theory in a critical manner. We are doing nothing more than acknowledging that there are some ideas or lines of argument that CoP theory is not fitted out to follow.

Successive explorations of CoP theory have highlighted several issues and phenomena that are of interest and importance for education researchers, but that do not have a place within CoP theory (for the most succinct summaries, see: Barton and Tusting, 2005; Hughes et al., 2007). Some of these have become quite common features of discussions about CoP theory more widely: the place of *power* is one of these (Boylan, 2010; Fox, 2000; Roberts, 2006) and indeed has been the subject of subsequent commentary from Wenger himself (Farnsworth et al., 2016), whilst others are less frequently voiced. CoP theory is incapable, we are told, of explaining the geographical or temporal relationships between different communities, or of generating sufficiently explicit accounts of the use of both the spoken and the written word – of particular importance in formal educational contexts where assessment and feedback practices (I shall discuss this in more depth in Chapter 7) are invariably bound up in different forms of writing (Hirst et al., 2004; Tapp, 2015). A full account of all such critiques of CoP theory would require an entirely separate book, but in addition to gender, some of those that are commonly discussed can be summarised as follows.

Power

CoP theory lacks conceptual tools for the explanation or analysis of power (control, conflict, stigma, and so forth) and consequently of resistance (refusal, disagreement, and so forth). How can we make sense of intergenerational conflicts between newcomers who seek to innovate and old-timers who are resistant to change? What if apprentices are deliberately blocked from the **legitimate peripheral practice** of the community – how will they then learn? What if old-timers are prevented from accessing new routines – new elements of the **shared repertoire**? Who polices the **boundaries** of the community – who or what is allowed on, and who or what is excluded, and on what grounds? Wenger's conception of inter-personal relationships within CoPs is too benign, perhaps even naive.

Response

One response is to use *theoretical plug-ins*, as discussed in Chapter 2. Fox (2000), in his account of power relations within Communities of Practice, draws on the work of philosopher and literary critic *Michel Foucault* (1926–84). Foucault's idea of power as being constantly created and recreated through unequal relations straightforwardly plugs in to CoP theory: the greater time served within the CoP that is enjoyed by the experienced older participant provides an 'automatic' inequality in relation to the newcomer, which therefore generates a power imbalance between the two participants. But this will not necessarily lead to conflict: whether or not such a power imbalance has negative or harmful consequences (as it were) will always depend on context – on the nature of the CoP in question, on the identities of the participants, and so forth. How power works within a CoP needs to be explained every time, not taken for granted. At the same time, it is worth noting that Wenger himself has responded to this longstanding critique of CoP theory:

[I]t is a learning theory, not a theory of power in general [...] if you want to look at the broader political context in which the local definition of competence is taking place, there are plenty of existing theories that address power at that level. So there is no need to reinvent them

Farnsworth et al., 2016: 153

Political economy

Further education colleges and adult education providers all exist in a relationship to a variety of governmental, industrial, and professional organisations. Some of these relate to the ways in which funding is provided. The *Education and Skills Funding Agency* provides one tranche of money for 16–19 provision, and a second for adults aged over 19. And there are separate funders for capital projects such as new builds and for college-based higher education. Others relate to curriculum: awarding bodies, professional organisations, and national training organisations all shape the daily practices of teachers and trainers. The Education and Training Foundation (ETF) sets the professional standards for the sector as a whole. How can we make sense of the relationships that must exist between an individual CoP or constellation of CoPs on the one hand, and the wider political and economic structures that exist in the world and that surround or influence what CoPs do?

Response

CoPs can answer some of these kinds of questions, but not others, and the main criterion for establishing which questions can be tackled remains the central tenet of the theory overall: that CoPs are social and cultural spaces within which learning happens. For example, if we want to explore the ways in which trainee FE teachers learn about the ETF professional standards, then we can start by thinking about the standards as being an example of an object or artefact (almost certainly in the form of a PDF file or a webpage) travelling across a constellation of Communities until it arrives at the teacher education CoP that we are interested in. If, during our research, we observe the professional standards being discussed during classes, written about in assignments, or referred to in reflective reports on teaching, then we can draw some tentative conclusions about how the professional standards are impacting on particular instances of learning within that specific teacher-education CoP – and perhaps across the wider teacher-education constellation that the CoP is an integral part of. But the wider political or institutional impetus that drives the professional standards is a matter for political/economic theories and/or theories of professionalism and professionalization, not for CoP theories (Tummons 2014a, 2014b, 2016).

A consideration of individual development

When new apprentices join a CoP for the first time and, through engaging in authentic practice, learn to become fuller participants, they are also undergoing a process of biological aging: the more time they spend in the community, the older they get. This means that as their membership continues, they are learning not only how to be fuller participants, but also how to be more mature adult members of society in general (Goodwin, 2007): how can we make sense of individual maturation – of growth – within CoP theory? How ought we to make sense of 'the particular attributes that individuals bring to cognitive processes' (Billett, 2007: 55)? Here, the argument is – in essence – that Lave and Wenger have thrown out the baby with the bathwater: by focussing so closely – one might even say relentlessly – on the social and the distributed (in terms of practice, of learning, of cognition, and of knowledge), the contribution of the individual – shaped by family, life history, or the simple fact of getting older and acquiring experience – has been at best overlooked.

Response

It is in the changing interests of Lave and Wenger (1991) and Wenger (1998) that these shifts of emphasis can be traced. For example, Wenger – at various points – discusses constructions of identity, memory, how adults can be role models, even histories of learning. But these topics are always brought back to the CoP as the focus for analysis. Identity is a consequence of participation in the community; memory is discussed only in contrast to physical artefacts such as documents; the potential for adults to serve as role models is restricted to old-timers as representatives of specific CoPs; and histories of learning are discussed in terms of practice within the lifecycle of the CoP. In the earlier book, by contrast, a more expansive understanding is hinted at (once again, this is an element of their argument that Lave and Wenger deal with in a frustratingly brief manner). Drawing on a range of wider sociological perspectives, Lave and Wenger suggest a theory of practice – of learning – that of necessity has to be situated within the historical development of the ongoing activity of society more generally but also taking account of individual decisions and capacities – of individual agency. 'Participation, at the core of our theory of learning, can be neither fully internalized [...] nor fully externalized' (1991: 51). There is, arguably, more still to be discussed here: certainly, a social practice theory of learning can help us make sense of a great many phenomena – but are we missing something by not focussing on the individual?

A critical understanding of language and literacy

A further gap in CoP theory is the relative lack of a series of theoretical tools to make sense of how people talk and how they write, and of how different kinds of language use can have different consequences or implications. The importance of discourse – written and spoken – is evident within CoP theory, but lacks specificity. For example, we know that discourses are important not only within individual CoPs, but across constellations, and that they can help people coordinate practice, or convince and persuade others about the merits or otherwise of differing perspectives. Discourses are not practices, however, but aspects of **shared repertoire** – material resources that can be used in a variety of contexts (Wenger, 1998: 129). But a definition of discourse is taken for granted within CoP theory, glossed over relatively swiftly. Within CoP theory, discourse is the resource that members use to describe and make sense of not only the practice of the community but the entire world (Wenger, 1998: 83). Language and literacy are self-evidently important, as the different vignettes from Wenger's own empirical research demonstrate. But *how* do they do what they do?

Response

Here once again we can use *theoretical plug-ins* (Chapter 2) to complement Wenger's theory. A first way forward would be to draw on research into language use. The research discussed by Karin Tusting, as already summarised in Chapter 3, would once again help us here (Tusting, 2005). Drawing on *linguistics* and on *discourse analysis*, she proposes that researchers pay close attention to language use within CoPs in terms of discourse, which Wenger does not define in full, but discourse analysts do. For example, if we listen in to talk within a CoP, are we listening to an argument, an explanation, or a description? Similarly, we might draw on research into different kinds of literacy. To do this, we need to move beyond narrow definitions of literacy that focus solely on literacy as a measure of being able to read and write or of being able to use specific bodies of knowledge or competence (phrases such as 'being computer literate' or even 'emotional literacy' spring to mind). Social practice accounts of literacy (*Literacy Studies*) can help us here (Barton, 1994; Barton and Hamilton, 1998). Literacy studies provides additional tools for thinking about how people use and talk about different kinds of written texts or artefacts that build on Wenger's ideas in a constructive manner, and I shall return to these ideas in Chapter 7 when discussing assessment and feedback.

In concluding this part of the discussion, it is important to note that these *absences* from CoP theory are not the only ones that scholars have identified. I have chosen these four quite deliberately in order to illustrate the simple fact that CoP theories cannot and should not be expected to do everything, but that if our research interests demand it, we can find additional ways to enrich the tools that Wenger provides. My argument here is that we should always remain respectful of CoP theory when doing so. Yes, there is an insufficient theorisation of power within CoP theory: then again, there is an insufficient theory of learning within discourse analysis. It is also important to recognise that on some occasions, discussing these theoretical absences provides more questions than answers. Looking for ways to explore literacies within CoPs can be found in a pretty straightforward way by using *literacy studies* theories (I shall return to these later). Looking for ways to account for individual development is a considerably more complex task – but we can nonetheless be aware of the problem even if we are not minded to find a solution: a critical use of CoP theory (or any other theoretical framework) means that we can acknowledge gaps or weaknesses whilst still using the theory in a robust and careful manner.

Looking for some answers

Up to this point, we have identified five areas of interest that are absent, or at best only briefly sketched, within CoP theory: gender; power; political economy; individual development; language and literacy. Having already discussed the research done by Helen Colley and colleagues in relation to gender, and having established that their account is *theoretically compatible* with a CoP-based account, we can now turn our attention to other examples from research literature to think about our other four areas for inquiry.

Power

Power relationships and imbalances can be found in a number of places – for example, between senior college leaders and teaching staff. They equally apply to relations between staff and students, and between researchers and those being researched. At a time when being research-informed or research-led is a live issue for teachers and trainers in the sector, the ethics of doing practitioner or action research are thrown into focus.

Liz Atkins has researched and written widely about one group of FE students that are certainly marginalised in a number of institutional and structural ways. Drawing on a commitment to social justice within both research and practice, she has discussed ways in which doing research *with* instead of *on* so-called 'disaffected' and 'disengaged' learners in FE can provide ways for them to be *given voice* – to have their own words and ideas expressed in an authentic manner, rather than simply being lost sight of within policy documents or research reports (Atkins, 2013). The social justice perspective adopted here derives from a commitment to finding out about the aspirations, lives, and experiences of these students on their own terms. Researching groups of level 1 students at two different FE colleges, Atkins details the complex range of backgrounds and needs that affect their lives and therefore their **trajectories** through formal education systems. Some have been excluded while at school, and others are looked after. Some have caring responsibilities and others have disabilities. Both of the colleges are situated within areas of economic and social disadvantage, in places where GCSE scores (using the five GCSEs benchmark) are below the national average. For the most part, students such as those written about by Atkins are viewed in negative terms – as being under-performing, but with no sense in policy documents of the varied and complex needs that such groups exhibit. They get described in terms of a *discourse of deficit* 'based on uncritical stereotypes of marginalised youth' (Atkins, 2013: 145). For Atkins, the first step has to be to ask these young people to tell her what they think she needs to know about their lives, their educational journeys, and their imagined futures.

From the standpoint of CoP theory, it is straightforward to imagine the different **trajectories** (as discussed in Chapter 2) of these young people. In terms of their experiences as FE students, they remain at a **peripheral** level due to the 'transitory' nature of their participation, near the **boundaries** of their communities, 'located at the bottom of a hierarchy of low-status vocational programmes in low-status institutions which form part of a broader system in which vocational education is held in lower esteem than academic education' (Atkins, 2013: 144, 145). Reflecting their ever-peripheral conditions, their learning will also be peripheral, and opportunities for fuller participation are made more difficult for them due to the structural and personal barriers that they face. But we need to look beyond CoP theory in order to appreciate the social justice imperative both of the research itself and of the ambition to shine a light on level 1 provision more broadly, as well as to make sense of the discourse of deficit that invariably surrounds students such as these.

Political economy

In writing this book, one of the issues that I hope to contribute to is *research literacy* – encouraging further and adult education teachers to use research and also conduct their own research as well. This is a feature of the current Education and Training Foundation (ETF) Professional Standards, which asks teachers to 'maintain and update your knowledge of educational research to develop evidence-based practice'. But if we turn our attention to those same professional standards (which, at the time of writing, are being revised by the ETF) then we find a perfect example of how the wider policy landscape has impacted the working practices of the sector over the course of several decades. It should be noted that although this discussion refers to the UK, parallell processes can be seen at work in Australia (Atkins and Tummons, 2017).

The first government report to highlight that the majority of teachers in further education colleges had no teaching qualifications was published in 1959. But despite further reports during the 1960s and 1970s, it was not until 1999 that the *Standards for Teaching and Supporting Learning in Further Education in England and Wales* were published by the now defunct *Further Education National Training Organisation* (FEnto). These new standards were mapped onto teaching qualifications, which remained voluntary, but were widely criticised by both academics and by Ofsted. FEnto was abolished and a new organisation, Lifelong Learning UK (LLUK) published a new set of standards in 2005 with a wider remit to include adult and community education. Completion of a now *compulsory* teaching qualification would then lead the teacher to work towards a new professional status – Qualified Teacher, Learning and Skills (QTLS) through compulsory membership of the Institute for Learning (IfL). These changes also failed to establish a coherent and uniform body of professional qualifications, and the anticipated regulation of continuing professional development (CPD) for teachers and trainers in lifelong learning also failed to materialise (Lucas, Nasta and Rogers, 2012; Orr, 2009). Just seven years later, further legislation rendered both qualifications and QTLS voluntary once again, the IfL was subsequently abolished, and in 2014 the ETF took responsibility for devising yet another professional framework. But throughout this 20-year period, teachers and trainers within the sector remain ambiguous in their awareness of and responses to the professional standards as public documents that purport to shape their professional lives (Tummons, 2016).

If we imagine a **constellation** of Communities of Practice for the further and adult education sectors, we can see professional standards (it doesn't matter which version) as part of the **shared repertoire**, shaping our professional lives in different ways. We can also see how the professional standards have travelled across a number of different **boundaries** – government departments, professional bodies, review boards – before finally arriving in colleges (we shall discuss boundary crossing in depth in Chapter 6). CoP theory lets us track the journeys that the standards have taken, but it doesn't help us explore the broader political and ideological arguments that have given them momentum. Should qualifications be voluntary or compulsory? Should they be delivered by universities or by awarding bodies? Should they be inspected by Ofsted? Answering these questions takes us away from CoP theory and into the study of educational policy more broadly (Coffield et al., 2008).

Individual development

At several points up to now, I have referred to the research of Stephen Billett, who over time has written extensively about learning in a variety of workplace contexts, including hairdressing salons. He has also drawn on this wider empirical work to critique elements of CoP theory – specifically, the ways in which the individual person is often lost sight of within the CoP literature. For Billett, 'humans are subject to emotion, inconsistency in responses, exhaustion, and inept responses that are not adequately accounted for in either cognitive or social constructivist accounts' (2007: 56). Certainly, this 'forgetting' of the individual was not something proposed by Lave and Wenger. If anything, they argued a quite opposite case: 'participation in social practice – subjective as well as objective – suggests a very explicit focus on the person, but as person-in-the-world, as member of a sociocultural community' (Lave and Wenger, 1991: 52). This idea that we need not only the community but also the person, the one relying on and supporting the other, is an example of a *relational* perspective – an idea found more widely in social research generally. In order to make sense of the community we need to understand the place of the individual within it – and *vice versa*. Lave and Wenger certainly wanted the focus to shift away from solely being on the individual, but they never meant for the individual to be subsumed by the CoP – but, like other elements of their work, this relational perspective got lost sight of.

Lave's subsequent work saw her return to critical ethnography and a very specific focus on apprenticeship learning, and Wenger's work has increasingly focused on corporate and organisational learning, but this is not to say that CoP theory cannot help us at all. Within the 1998 framework, **identity** is aligned to **practice** in a number of ways. Our identities can be shaped by **inter-generational encounters** with younger and older CoP members as well as by what we learn and where. More importantly, Wenger states that identity 'is not confined to specific periods of life, like adolescence, or to specific settings, like the family' (1998: 163). But they are still part of identity nonetheless. Wenger does not remove them from consideration, but neither does he account fully for their explanatory potential. But it would nonetheless be a mistake to try to draw on individual psychological models of learning in response to this. The gap that we have identified is not so much about whether we should return to an individual model of cognition of the kind that Lave (1988) in particular rejects so forcefully (as discussed in Chapter 2), but whether or not we need to think a bit more about how individual people work and behave within a CoP, how much freedom of action or autonomy they enjoy, how CoPs might shift in order to accommodate individuals, and so forth. Wenger provides us with tools for thinking about how the CoP shapes the person: what about the person who shapes the CoP?

Concepts of individual autonomies and freedoms, or *agencies*, within different kinds of social environments have been explored in depth by a number of sociological researchers. A discussion of *agency* could fill a much larger book than the one that you are reading now, so here I will refer to the definition provided by the sociologist Anthony Giddens: 'agency concerns events of which an individual is a perpetrator [...] whatever happened would not have happened if that individual had not intervened' (Giddens, 1984: 9). There are other definitions, and other writers who would disagree with Giddens. But the key issue remains that agency is under-explored within CoP theory and ideas about agency from wider sociological research do provide a useful way to think about this. For example, the *Transforming Learning Cultures in Further Education* project (mentioned above) drew explicitly on the theoretical framework of French sociologist Pierre Bourdieu in order to explore the relationships between different sites of learning (referred to in the project as *learning cultures*) and the individual students found within them: 'individuals influence are part of learning cultures just as learning cultures influence and are part of individuals' (James and Biesta, 2007: 29).

Interlude: the learning journeys of vocational teachers

Adeline Goh has researched and written about the professional learning of vocational teachers using a range of social practice theories (Goh, 2013, 2015). In the second of these papers, she argues that CoP theory 'inadvertently undermines the role of individuals in their learning' and that social theory more broadly has a tendency to 'disregard individual learning and individual biographies' (Goh, 2015: 681). Through following the trajectories of several trainee teachers, as they travel between the workplaces where they are teachers and the institutions where they are learners, Goh raises questions about the nature of the apprentices' peripheral trajectories within CoPs. One teacher within her study felt marginalized in the workplace, but thanks to good mentoring she was given the chance to observe teaching, then to co-teach, with opportunities to model practice throughout. A second teacher was required to work alongside colleagues who expected her to know more than she did. She received no mentoring and remained in a more marginal, peripheral, position. Goh concludes that closer attention needs to be paid to the detail of individual student biographies.

Language and literacy

It is important to recognise that CoP theory does provide useful conceptual tools for thinking critically and carefully about how text-based artefacts are created and used. Of greatest relevance to this discussion are **transparency** and **communicative ability. Transparency** relates to the interplay between the use of any artefact and the understanding of why it is important or significant. As someone's participation becomes more full, so artefacts become more transparent to the practitioner (Lave and Wenger, 1991: 101–2). The more we learn, the more easily we can use the artefacts. In part, this is simply because we know more and therefore we can do more stuff. And in part it is because as we know more, we are better able to understand the full significance or utility of any of the resources of the community, including texts. Wenger develops this further through the concept of the **communicative ability** of an artefact (1998: 64). **Communicative ability** rests on two factors: the extent to which a CoP member understands the significance of the artefact as a consequence of the extent or depth of her/his participation; and the extent to which an artefact manages to embody meaning: simply put, does the text make sense to the reader?

We are off to a good start, but if we also draw on social practice theories of literacy – *literacy studies* – we can take our analysis further (Barton, 1994; Barton and Hamilton, 1998). There are a few concepts that we might use. First, we can think about the ways in which people read and then make meaning from a text. From a literacy studies perspective, a text or document does not have a single unarguable meaning. Instead, the ways in which a text is understood will always be shaped by the person who is reading them – more specifically, by their experience, their prior knowledge, their familiarity with the style or type of text, and so forth. We can also think about how some ways of writing and speaking are more powerful than others. For example, there are specific ways in which students are *expected* to write assignments, and in which FE college programme leaders are *expected* to write self-assessment reports. Some forms of literacy are privileged – they are powerful or *dominant*; others are everyday *vernacular* literacies that are less highly valued in formal contexts.

Even the instructions provided on, and the shape and design of, forms and official documents – the boxes that need to be filled in on an assessment report, for example – can have consequences for how they are used. Mary Hamilton's research into the ways in which Individual Learning Plans (ILPs) were used in colleges delivering Skills for Life programmes (the adult and literacy curriculum established by the New Labour government in 2001) provides a good example. In her research, Hamilton demonstrated how the practices of filling in the ILP forms at the start of each new course were a site of tension. On the one hand, tutors wanted the process to be meaningful and helpful for the student. But on the other hand, they felt that they had to fill the ILPs in order to 'hit the right buttons' (Hamilton, 2009: 238) so that they were completed in the way that college auditors and inspectors demanded. ILPs are not only artefacts for assessment, but also artefacts for quality assurance and inspection, and these at-times conflicting demands shape the ways in which they are used by both tutors and students – a model case for the use of *literacy studies* alongside CoP theory.

Some conclusions

Any theoretical framework has limits. CoP theory can be stretched and reshaped a bit, but there are some places that it can't go without help. In this chapter, I have focussed on some of the more commonly found things that have attracted critique from a number of researchers and writers – critique that is not always fully justified, I suggest, but that nonetheless deserves a response. In doing so, I have drawn on prior research in order to give examples of different ways through which these critiques might be addressed. The researchers whom I have referred to in this chapter are not setting out to either dismantle or build on CoP theory: rather, they have drawn on other perspectives that are sympathetic to a CoP approach and that we can, therefore, use alongside CoP theory in order to unpack and understand those issues and problems that Wenger (1998) cannot reach. As ever, the further and adult education sector is under-represented in the literature, but the studies and authors referred to here have, between them, produced much work that is worth pursuing for anyone who wishes to engage with meaningful research about the sector. Much of the work cited was carried out in collaboration with representatives from the sector, and as such is of particular value if we are to give voice to students and teachers who oftentimes are not properly heard.

References

Atkins, L. (2013) Researching 'with' not 'on': engaging marginalised learners in the research process. *Research in Post-Compulsory Education* 18 (1–2) 143–158. doi:10.1080/13596748.2013.755853.

Atkins, L. and Tummons, J. (2017) Professionalism in vocational education: international perspectives. *Research in Post-Compulsory Education* 22(3) 355–369. DOI:doi:10.1080/13596748.2017.1358517.

Barton, D. (1994) *Literacy: An Introduction to the Ecology of Written Language.* Oxford: Blackwell.

Barton, D. and Hamilton, M. (1998) *Local Literacies: Reading and Writing in One Community.* London: Routledge.

Barton, D. and Tusting, K. (eds.) (2005) *Beyond Communities of Practice: Language, Power and Social Context.* Cambridge: Cambridge University Press.

Billett, S. (2007) Including the missing subject: placing the personal within the community. In Hughes, J., Jewson, N. and Unwin, L. (eds) *Communities of Practice: Critical Perspectives.* London: Routledge. 55–67.

Boylan, M. (2010) Ecologies of participation in school classrooms. *Teaching and Teacher Education*, 26 (1) 61–70. doi:10.1016/j.tate.2009.08.005.

Coffield, F., Edward, S., Finlay, I., Hodgson, A., Spours, K., and Steer, R. (2008) *Improving Learning, Skills and Inclusion: The impact of policy on post-compulsory education.* London: Routledge.

Colley, H., James, D., Diment, K., and Tedder, M. (2003) Learning as becoming in vocational education and training: class, gender and the role of vocational habitus. *Journal of Vocational Education and Training* 55 (4) 471–498. doi:10.1080/13636820300200240.

Farnsworth V., Kleanthous I., and Wenger-Trayner, E. (2016) Communities of Practice as a Social Theory of Learning: a Conversation with Etienne Wenger. *British Journal of Educational Studies*, 64 (2) 139–160. doi:10.1080/00071005.2015.1133799.

Fox, S. (2000) Communities of practice, Foucault and actor-network theory. *Journal of Management Studies* 37 (6) 853–867. doi:10.1111/1467-6486.00207.

Giddens, A. (1984) *The Constitution of Society: outline of the theory of structuration.* Berkeley: University of California Press.

Goh, A.Y.S. (2013) The significance of social relationships in learning to become a vocational and technical education teacher. *Studies in Continuing Education* 35 (3) 366–378. doi:10.1080/0158037X.2013.770390.

Goh, A.Y.S. (2015) An individual learning journey: learning as becoming a vocational teacher. *International Journal of Lifelong Education* 34 (6) 680–695. doi:10.1080/02601370.2015.1096311.

Goodwin, J. (2007) The transition to work and adulthood: becoming adults via communities of practice. In Hughes, J., Jewson, N., and Unwin, L. (eds.) *Communities of Practice: critical perspectives.* London: Routledge. 96–108.

Hamilton, M. (2009). Putting words in their mouths: the alignment of identities with system goals through the use of Individual Learning Plans. *British Educational Research Journal*, 35(2), 221–242. doi:10.1080/01411920802042739.

Hirst, E., Henderson, R., Allan, M., Bode, J., and Kocatepe, M. (2004). Repositioning academic literacy: Charting the emergence of a community of practice. *The Australian Journal of Language and Literacy*, 27 (1), 66–80.

Hughes, J., Jewson, N. and Unwin, L. (eds.) (2007) *Communities of Practice: critical perspectives.* London: Routledge.

James, D. and Biesta, G. (2007) *Improving Learning Cultures in Further Education.* London: Routledge.

Lave, J. (1988) *Cognition in Practice: Mind, Mathematics and Culture in Everyday Life.* Cambridge: Cambridge University Press.

Lave, J. and Wenger, E. (1991) *Situated Learning: Legitimate Peripheral Participation.* Cambridge: Cambridge University Press.

Lucas, N., Nasta, T., and Rogers, L. (2012) From fragmentation to chaos? The regulation of initial teacher training in further education. *British Educational Research Journal* 38 (4) 677–695. doi:10.1080/01411926.2011.576750.

Orr, K. (2009) Performativity and professional development: the gap between policy and practice in the English further education sector. *Research in Post Compulsory Education* 14 (4) 479–489. doi:10.1080/13596740903361016.

Paechter, C. (2003) Masculinities and femininities as communities of practice. *Women's Studies International Forum* 26 (1) 69–77. doi:10.1016/S0277-5395(02)00356-4.

Roberts, J. (2006) Limits to communities of practice. *Journal of Management Studies* 43 (3) 623–637. doi:10.1111/j.1467-6486.2006.00618.x.

Tapp, J. (2015) Framing the curriculum for participation: a Bernsteinian perspective on academic literacies. *Teaching in Higher Education* 20 (7), 711–722. doi:10.1080/13562517.2015.1069266.

Tummons, J. (2014a) The textual representation of professionalism: problematising professional standards for teachers in the UK lifelong learning sector. *Research in Post-Compulsory Education* 19 (1): 33–44. doi:10.1080/13596748.2014.872918.

Tummons, J. (2014b) Professional standards in teacher education: tracing discourses of professionalism through the analysis of textbooks. *Research in Post-Compulsory Education* 19 (4): 417–432. doi:10.1080/13596748.2014.955634.

Tummons, J. (2016). 'Very positive' or 'vague and detached'? Unpacking ambiguities in further education teachers' responses to professional standards in England. *Research in Post-Compulsory Education* 21 (4): 346–359. doi:10.1080/13596748.2016.1226589.

Tusting, K. (2005) Language and Power in Communities of Practice. In Barton, D. and Tusting, K. (eds) *Beyond Communities of Practice: Language, Power and Social Context*. Cambridge: Cambridge University Press. 36–54.

Wenger, E. (1998) *Communities of Practice: Learning, Meaning and Identity*. Cambridge: Cambridge University Press.

6 Constellations, boundaries, and brokers

Introduction

In this sixth chapter, I am going to draw on a fictional life history of a college lecturer (well, partly fictional – many parts of her story are based on real events) in order to unpack the different ways by which we can make sense of the flows of traffic – of artefacts, emails, people, things, routines, actions, and so forth – that generate and then sustain connections between different Communities of Practice. Sometimes these CoPs are closely aligned in terms of what they do, and at other times they are more distinct, but CoPs are always in communication with other CoPs, and are never isolated.

A not-unusual day in a busy FE college

Picture this: you are an English lecturer in a busy college, and you have worked there for several years. Most of your time is spent teaching English for Speakers of Other Languages (ESOL) courses – a bit of a way away from your background as an English Literature student at the local university, and from the A-level English classes that you first taught on as a part-time, hourly paid tutor. Happily for your mortgage – if not for your love of literature – the ESOL provision at the college is very busy and there are more than enough courses to justify a permanent contract, and with it a permanent desk in a large shared office (something that the part-time tutors rarely get). With a workload topped-up with a continuing small amount of provision for adult learners doing A-level English, and some course management responsibilities, your working week is certainly busy. Like many other colleges, external financial pressures have required changes to the curriculum and also changes to the structure of the college. Responding to recent Ofsted inspections is also adding to the general workload across the institution. The college is arguably short-staffed, although it takes time for new colleagues to be appointed, and with a small number of people signed off from work due to sickness – and in one case, stress – it's not uncommon for you to be asked to cover other classes. That's how you ended up doing some regular teaching on the initial teacher education (ITE) programme (that part-time MA in Education came in useful after

DOI: 10.4324/9781003252566-6

all). But when you were asked to cover a level 3 BTEC Business Studies class, you stopped in your tracks. How can you teach a session for a course that you know nothing about?

Luckily, you have been asked to cover for the *Developing a Marketing Campaign* unit. This is a core unit for all students – certificate and diploma – and the *market research methods and use* segment is easy for you to cover. All you need to do is adapt some of the research methods materials that you covered for your MA: how to use quantitative and qualitative data; doing interviews, observations, focus groups, and surveys; validity, reliability, and sufficiency of the data collected. Translating these topics from education to business research won't take too long, and you'll be able to speak about them and run a workshop activity with confidence, based on the simple fact that you know the subjects well. The lesson goes really well, and you aren't even thrown off balance when one of the college vice principals decides to come in to the session as part of a walkthrough observation exercise. The VP is so impressed, in fact, with the way that you ran the class that they ask that you cover some more of the BTEC Business programme over the following weeks. But this won't be so easy. Reworking some research methods materials was a little time consuming, but what do you know about developing a marketing campaign? What is a PESTLE analysis? What is guerrilla marketing? How do you manage a campaign budget and make sure that it is sustainable? You've been given full access to the course website, resources, and files, but they are unfamiliar in look and feel. This is going to be far outside your expertise and experience.

Constellations, border crossings, and multimembership: tracing a path across multiple Communities of Practice

A *nexus* is another word for a connecting point that links two or more things in the same place. Our fictional tutor (in fact based on an amalgamation of real-life stories from two FE tutors), as she walks around college trying to work out how to find the time to prepare for her BTEC Business classes whilst still teaching ESOL, finds herself at a *nexus of practices* – a point where several different practices are all pushing and pulling her at the same time. Within the **constellation** of CoPs that make up the college where she works, her well-established and experienced position within the ESOL CoP stands in stark contrast to her sudden arrival as a newcomer in the BTEC Business CoP. She is standing at a **nexus of multimembership** (Wenger, 1998: 158).

Our tutor has travelled across a number of different CoPs, following different **trajectories** (as discussed in Chapter 2) up to now. Having started out as a university student doing English, she will have been a member of an English-at-university CoP, following a **peripheral** and then **outbound trajectory**. Her time in that community was by definition always going to be temporary, covering her time as a student. But membership of that community has helped her to become a member of at least two others: the CoP of the A-level evening classes for adults, and the CoP of the ESOL programme. Or, to put it another way, she had to be a member of the first

CoP before she was able to become a member of the next two (Lemke, 1997; see also our discussion about new patterns of multi-membership in Chapter 3). In different ways, she has been able to translate elements of her practice from the university CoP to the others. Some of this translation relates to specialist knowledge – to expertise – of course, but some also relates to less explicit ways of knowing. For example: the A-level students will have to do a close reading of *Regeneration*, a novel about the First World War, and this is just the kind of close analysis of a text that out tutor was doing throughout her degree.

Now, our tutor – like every university student – also developed a range of key and transferable skills during her time at university, especially in terms of spoken and written communication, and these have proved helpful when giving feedback to her students, and when explaining things in class. But developing communication skills whilst studying for a degree in English Literature doesn't fully equip you to teach ESOL – that's what the *Certificate in Teaching English to Speakers of Other Languages* (CELTA) is for (other specialist ESOL programmes are available). Our tutor had chosen to do a CELTA course when she couldn't find a full-time job as an English Literature tutor. Some of the CELTA curriculum was very familiar to her, and easy to pick up – especially in relation to word meaning and use in context (this is referred to as *lexis*). The stuff on how the different components of a word can be changed to make another word, such as changing from cat to bat (this is referred to as *phonology*) was new, but she soon got the hang of it. Phonology and lexis are two examples of specific language that make up part of the **shared repertoire** of the ESOL community. And the time spent discussing lesson planning and choosing and evaluating resources was very easy, because she had already done a module on this for her PGCE in post-compulsory education and training (PCET), which she had studied on a part-time basis whilst teaching evening classes.

Let's sum up. Our tutor's journey – as far as this analysis is concerned – started with her university degree, on the basis of which she was able to start teaching evening classes. Supporting herself through collecting a series of part-time hourly paid contracts was not sustainable, so she decided to obtain a teaching qualification in order to facilitate a move to a permanent contract. But it was her subsequent decision to study CELTA that really helped, because the college where she worked needed ESOL teachers more than it needed English A-level teachers, and the nature of the funding structure was such that the college could appoint someone to specialise in ESOL on a permanent contract. She only teaches adult classes as well because there's capacity in her workload: if the ESOL numbers grow again, the A-level evening classes will have to go.

A nexus of multimembership: identity and reconciliation

Multimembership of a number of CoPs – they might all belong to the same **constellation**, but this is not automatic – consists of two elements: identity, and reconciliation (Wenger, 1998: 158–61). When we talk about **identity**, we have to remember that our identities as people in the world are shaped by all sorts of things, including our differing levels of membership of different CoPs. We are different when we are in different places. We speak, behave, and even dress differently at work and at home. We might speak differently to different groups of students depending on their ages, their level of study, whether they are full-time or part-time. But we do not build walls between these different parts of our identities. We might tell a story about our children, say, as a way of illustrating a point that we are trying to get across to our learners. We might reflect on how a session went with one group of students and then adapt the resources when sitting down with the next group. On one day, we might be working with a longstanding group of students, teaching a curriculum that we know inside-out because we have been running the modules in question for several years and our trajectory is that of the **insider**. And on the next day, we might be working with a new group in a new subject area, on an **inbound** trajectory that reflects our relative lack of professional experience. But all of these CoPs and all of these trajectories stay separate, even though they all work on us, and we are members of them, at the same time. We borrow from one, travel from one to the other, talk differently in some than on others, and so forth. This is what we mean when we talk about our identities as resting on multimembership (Wenger, 1998).

Sometimes, moving between CoPs or borrowing from one CoP and giving to another can be quite straightforward, especially if the CoPs in question are closely aligned. **Alignment** between different CoPs helps them join together in ways that allow the practices of those CoPs to expand and travel (Wenger, 1998: 178–81). At other times, however, we may find ourselves occupying positions that are contradictory, or that might push us into an action or a process that makes sense from the standpoint of one CoP, but is less agreeable or appropriate to another. On occasions such as this, our identity relies on **reconciliation work**. Sometimes, this might happen from the standpoint of a single trajectory within a single CoP. For example, when I worked as a teacher-educator in FE colleges, I sometimes had to make decisions about what to focus on in the classroom based on external pressures from Ofsted. Balancing the academic content of the course with the audit requirements of Ofsted demanded a process of reconciliation between my identity as a teacher educator – an autonomous professional working to professional standards – and an employee of a college that on an institutional basis had to plan for and respond to a cycle of inspections. At other times, reconciliation work is required in order to resolve tensions that come about as a result of being a member of two (or more) CoPs that pull in different, conflicting directions. As a teacher educator, I was part of the *Higher Education in Further Education* (HE in FE) provision (this is now usually referred to as College-Based Higher Education – CBHE). On the one hand, from a university perspective I was expected to keep up to date with the literature and scholarship that underpinned the curriculum; but from an FE college perspective I was not given any more planning and preparation time than any other member of teaching staff. I only resolved this problem by moving to another FE college where the HE manager was more sympathetic to the time needed to plan for university-level programmes.

Let us now return to our fictional tutor. Drawing on several concepts from CoP theory, we can therefore say that she occupies a nexus of multimembership that rests on different trajectories within several Communities of Practice that are part of the same constellation although differently aligned, and that she engages in ongoing reconciliation work as she builds and sustains her identity. If we consider her journey from student to classroom practitioner we find her travelling through several CoPs:

1   An English student at university, leading to...
2   A part-time hourly paid tutor, at the same time as being...
3   A PGCE (PCET) student, which was followed by being...
4   A CELTA student, leading to...
5   A full-time ESOL college lecturer, with a course leadership role, and maintaining a small amount of evening-class teaching.

Over time, she has followed several qualitatively different types of **trajectory** – sometimes peripheral and outbound (as a student) and sometimes inbound and leading to insider (as a full-time lecturer, latterly with responsibilities for course leadership). The nature of the trajectory does not necessarily depend on time – the CELTA course took only three months whereas the PGCE (PCET) course took two years, both on a part-time basis – but on the nature or quality of participation. Sometimes, access to one CoP has only been possible thanks to previous membership of a different CoP but this does not mean that those CoPs are overlapping. Rather, it is in the ways that the **boundaries** of these different CoPs are maintained, that we can find out the terms and conditions by which new, peripheral, members can be admitted – and by extension, the reasons given for keeping other people out.

Boundaries: defining the limits of a Community of Practice

We have already spent a little time in the company of CoP **boundaries** and **boundary objects**. In Chapter 1, I gave an example from my own research of one of the ways in which the members of the horticulture and animal care departments at one land-based college maintained the boundary between themselves: through humour. The horticulture staff referred to the animal care staff as the 'bunny strokers' who in turn called the horticulture staff the 'flower pickers'.

In Chapter 2, we read about boundary trajectories – the trajectories of those people who choose or are required to participate at the boundaries of communities, and who never set out – or gain permission – to engage in full practice on an inbound or insider trajectory.

In Chapter 3, I discussed a research paper that explored the relationships between teachers and museum educators, and the ways in which museums generate boundary objects to help the teachers and their students get to know more about what the museum is about (Herne, 2006).

In Chapter 4 we encountered the key concept of the **Learning Architecture** as a way of building the foundations for a CoP to emerge. Remembering that no CoP is isolated from any other, or indeed from the world at large, we read about how the links between the global and the local are facilitated in part through boundary crossings.

And in Chapter 5, there were several references to the ways in which objects, resources, or ideas, as well as people, might cross boundaries between different CoPs.

But we now need to pull all of these strands together so that we can be clear about what we mean when we talk about the boundaries of a CoP, about how – exactly – people and stuff gain permission to cross over these boundaries, and about how one CoP might thereby shape the practices of another to a greater or lesser degree.

Boundaries: what marks out the boundaries of a CoP?

In Chapter 1, the key CoP components of **mutual engagement, joint enterprise**, and **shared repertoire** were introduced. And these are important for us, because it is in how these three things are done that we can discern the boundaries of the community in question. A CoP boundary is not a single thing in and of itself, and cannot straightforwardly be reduced to a physical entity. Yes, a carpentry and joinery department can be seen as a Community of Practice, but it is not the fact that you would have to pass through a specific set of double doors to get to it that makes it a Community with a tightly defined boundary. It is the nature of the practices of the community that make it distinct. What people do, what tools and techniques they use, how they speak and write about what they do, how they might dress, and so forth – these are the things that the rest of us can see and hear that set the Community of Carpentry and Joinery Practice apart from the other technical, vocational, and academic communities that make up the constellation of one particular FE college.

In some CoPs, therefore, it will be in the ways that people dress that membership can be most straightforwardly identified: the construction staff and students will wear overalls, and the air cabin crew staff and students will wear uniform. There's no uniform for ESOL classes, but there is a specialist vocabulary ('lexis', 'phonology'), part of the shared repertoire of the Community of ESOL Practice, that helps them stand out in just the same way as do the workbooks or resources that the students are working with. Many of the tools that might be found in a cycle mechanics' workshop will be the same as those found in a car mechanics' workshop, but some will be quite distinct to one or the other. The differences between two CoPs based around academic subjects, by contrast, might take a little longer to tease apart. At first look, an A-level class in sociology probably won't seem particularly different to an A-level class in law (especially if there are lots of students doing both subjects – they are often recommended as a combination in prospectuses), unless the college in question has provided 'base rooms' for both that can then be adorned with posters and suchlike that reflect the subject area. But a more fine-grained observation will highlight different resources on desks, different examples of terminology, and so forth.

Crossing borders: who are the people who cross boundaries, and why do they do so?

The obvious answer to the question 'who crosses the boundaries of a CoP, and why?' is: anybody who wants or is required to become a member of the Community of Practice. Boundary crossing takes place irrespective of the trajectory that the newcomer might find themselves on or aspire to in the future. The particular trajectory that they imagine themselves on relates to the 'why'. A newcomer to the Community of Sports Science Practice in a further education college who aspires to working in a professional setting such as a leisure centre will set off on a trajectory that will always be **peripheral** and **outbound**, undertaking membership of this community solely to enable access to a different one, in industry, in due course. But a newcomer who has come from the industry and is seeking to retrain as a teacher will follow a different, **inbound** trajectory. For the new teacher, their trajectory is defined in part by their identity as already shaped by their past membership(s) of industrial CoPs, and by their **reconciliation work** in learning to balance what they have learned from industry with the specifications of a college curriculum that will require more precise and standardised ways of working. They will be more familiar with local practices, shortcuts, and workarounds, which are common features of work, rather than study, and of which line managers and supervisors may well be entirely unaware [Belfiore et al., 2004]) There are also some people who are long-standing, senior members of the CoP who nonetheless do not hold a central position or follow an **insider** trajectory. Instead, they follow – either through choice or through being asked – a **boundary** trajectory, and their practice is deliberately located at the boundaries of one or more CoPs, and is characterised by **brokering** (Wenger, 1998: 108–13).

   Brokering is a very specific element of the wider work of any Community of Practice, and also something that is commonly found. It refers to any of the work that is done by community members who are responsible for making connections between different CoPs. This is *not* the same as multimembership, however. Multimembership specifically relates to the ways in which being a member of one or more CoPs mediates one's identity – for example, in how an apprentice on day release might carry ways of knowing and being between their college course and their work placement. Brokering involves always being at the boundaries of CoPs, building connections between them in order to facilitate coordinated effort, introduce the practices of one into the repertoire of another so as to enable a new form of learning, represent the practices of one CoP to the members of another, and so forth – a kind of 'import–export' process (Wenger, 1998: 109). A college-based work placement coordinator is a good example of a broker and represents the interests of the college when visiting employers and preparing the ground for future students who will travel on a regular basis between two CoPs – that of their college course, and that of their workplace.

Crossing borders: how is it done?

Membership of a Community of practice is not a given, nor an entitlement. Even a *weakly framed* CoP (Boud and Middleton, 2003) asks something of its members as well as providing affordances for participation in return. There is an unavoidable gate-keeping aspect to a Community of Practice that can help or hinder border crossing. Border crossings can be facilitated in different ways, depending on the nature of the person or people who want to gain entry. A *tightly framed* CoP with a very clear and coherent **joint enterprise** will look for quite specific things from newcomers. A straightforward example of this would be the entry requirements that are attached to many further and adult education courses, although these might be enacted in very different ways. A typical entry from a prospectus for applicants for a T-level course in construction design, surveying, and planning might say something like: 'entry requirements for this course are 4 or 5 GCSE subjects at grade 4 or above including Maths and/or English'. By contrast, the admissions requirements for a Spanish language course run by a community education service run by a local council might be less specific, for example: 'This is the second term of a beginners' course so it is expected that you have completed at least one term of Spanish learning recently. Alternatively, if you studied Spanish a long time ago and you still remember how the present tense in Spanish works, then this course is suitable for you also. If you're not sure if this course is the right level for you, click here to use our online level checker.' Both of these, in their different ways, are assessment decisions, and rely on the assessments in question being trustworthy: we shall return to this in the following chapter.

Not everyone who is looking to join a CoP in further and adult education is doing so in order to be a student, of course: our fictional tutor from the start of the chapter has, over time, joined several CoPs as both student and teacher. Other people look to gain access to a community for only very specific reasons that are not connected to a desire to engage in practice as a peripheral or full member, but simply as **visitors** (Wenger, 1998: 112). Visiting a CoP is a specific kind of **boundary encounter** that might be one-off, discrete events, or part of a longer-standing relationship between two or more CoPs that are either already part of a constellation where practice can be shared, or where greater collaboration is the outcome of the visit. For example, when an external verifier from an awarding body travels to a college, they are representing the interests, concerns, and practices of the awarding body that they represent: this is a boundary encounter that stays at the boundary of the college CoP. But when staff from one college attend another college in order to see how that college delivers a particular course, for example, then a more immersive visit has been established. Exchanges such as this tend to be one-way, however – a mutual exchange of practices requires visits in both directions.

Boundary objects: what can artefacts do when they travel between communities?

Any element of a **shared repertoire** – a tool, a routine, a document – can travel between Communities of Practice in a manner analogous to the ways in which people do. As we saw in Chapter 4, CoPs are simultaneously global and local to differing degrees, and regularly adopt and customize materials or processes from other, more-or-less distant, communities. But there are other kinds of artefacts that help to build connections between different communities *without* being adopted in this way. To describe these, Wenger draws on the work of Susan Leigh Star, a sociologist of science and technology who introduced the concept of the **boundary object** (Star and Griesemer, 1989; Wenger, 1998: 106–08). Boundary objects can, in effect, act as containers of meaning or practice that can then travel around between different CoPs, without being permanently absorbed into one of them. In this way, they can help with the circulation of ideas, practices, processes, and so forth.

According to Star, there are four types of boundary object, although this was never intended to be a definitive list (Star and Griesemer, 1989: 410–11):

1   *Repositories.* A repository is something like a library, or a museum. They consist simply of piles of objects (of whatever kind the repository is about) that have been grouped together using some kind of organising or indexing system, to help people find the thing that they need. The website for the Education and Training Foundation is an example of a repository; a college learning resource centre is a more complex example.
2   *Ideal types.* An ideal type (where ideal means 'most suitable' rather than 'perfect') is any object that is not an accurate representation of one specific thing but a generalised abstraction. An ideal type is vague and lacking in specificity, but can be adopted to a specific context relatively easily. A resuscitation manikin used in first aid training is an example of an ideal type – it doesn't specifically look like any particular person, but instead serves to represent people generally.
3   *Coincident boundaries.* Objects that have coincident boundaries have the same boundaries as each other but different contents. For example, a group of construction students might have a number of different floor plans for the same building, showing the work to be done by different trades – so there will be plumbing drawings, electrical and lighting drawings, and so on.
4   *Standardised forms.* A standardised form is an object that has been constructed in such a way as to allow for communication across separate communities. Once the form has been designed, information will always be organised on the form in a consistent way, and this helps the form to travel between different locations, carrying with it the information in question.

Boundary objects help all kinds of things travel between different CoPs: materials, routines, forms of expression, messages, bodies of knowledge, codified information, and so on. Their defining characteristic, irrespective of type, is that they do not settle – either temporarily or permanently, into the CoP to which they have travelled. Their job is as a transmitter or conveyor of whatever it is that is being transmitted or conveyed. As such, in order to make sure that the message gets through properly, boundary objects are often – though by no means always – accompanied by people. For example, a *Statement of Special Educational Needs* is a **boundary object**, specifically an example of a standardised form. The format that a statement takes has been designed in such a way that a specific body of required information can be transmitted without any loss to, say, a module leader who will then be responsible for ensuring that the necessary study support has been put into place. But a focus on special educational needs (SEN) is not a compulsory element of most initial teacher education programmes, and not every tutor has experience in accommodating SEN students. They might be able to read the statement, but they may not appreciate fully what it implies or entails – what it *means*. But if the statement can be accompanied on some way by a person who can provide extra guidance and detail, any potential problem of communication can be resolved.

Interlude: researching boundary crossings in vocational education

Selena Chan is a researcher based in Aotearoa New Zealand (where tertiary education provision is quite similar to that of the UK – see also Kamp, 2019), and has published widely on different aspects of vocational and craft expertise. In a paper published ten years ago (at the time of writing) she described her research with a group of new tutors from a range of vocational areas – automotive, carpentry, catering, electrical installation, painting and decorating, and plumbing – with a specific focus on the extent to which they managed their transformations from 'expert trade workers to effective trades tutors' (Chan, 2012: 409). She conceptualised these processes as examples of **boundary crossings**, and found that in a majority of cases, the trade workers – already long-standing members of their vocational CoPs – expressed a reluctance to be identified as a tutor first and as a trade expert next. Instead, they preferred to sustain their deep attachments to their trades. Chan concluded that new forms of professional induction and mentoring, modelled on CoPs, would provide a possible way forward for sustaining the changes in identity that moving from trade to education would require.

A not-unusual day in a busy FE college, revisited

In returning to the story of our FE tutor as she hurriedly prepares to teach on the BTEC Business Studies course, we might instead use this subtitle: *one college lecturer's nexus of multimembership through boundary crossing within a constellation of Communities of Practice* – so long as we are happy to use the jargon. If we go back to her overall professional journey (from university student to part-time tutor to PGCE and then CELTA student to ESOL lecturer and course manager), we are now in a position to trace that same journey through using the different components of CoP theory that we have discussed up to this point in the chapter.

An English student at university

When she was at university, our tutor was a student in an English department – or, better, she was a member of a Community of English Practice. When describing university CoPs, some authors make a distinction between the teaching and the research functions of a university department whereas other authors combine the two: both options have their merits as well as their limitations, and either approach will work here (Tummons, 2018). Like FE colleges, universities can be seen as **constellations** of CoPs, sometimes joining together in order to accomplish particular cross-departmental actions such as innovative research projects that combine distinct academic departments (law and biology, for example, or medicine and history), and for the rest of the time working within their own disciplinary boundaries. In FE colleges, where research is only seldom found and usually either led by a small group of individuals on an informal basis or concentrated on college-based higher education (CBHE) staff, similar cross-departmental actions might be found in things such as key skills provision that can be rolled out across different vocational areas.

At university, our tutor – then a student – followed an **outbound, peripheral trajectory**. She was never going to become an academic – she didn't want to do that – and so once her course was finished and she had been awarded her degree certificate (we will discuss certification and assessment more broadly in the next chapter) she was able to use her qualifications to gain employment. A degree certificate is an example of a **boundary artefact**, carrying a particular kind of information about one community to another. In this instance, the degree certificate carries a message that says something (rightly or wrongly – we will address this in Chapter 7) about the knowledge, intelligence, capacity, and so forth of the student who holds it. Our ex-student, accompanied by her degree certificate (or it might be the other way around) provides a sufficient rationale for her to be allowed to engage in **border crossing** – and thereby gain admittance to the fringes of the college.

A part-time hourly paid tutor

The role of the part-time tutor can be complicated. On the one hand, part-time tutors often feel that they live and work at the edges of organisations, at risk of being at best overlooked if not forgotten about by managers and leaders; on the other, they nonetheless occupy a crucial, invariably well-defined role that rests on a commitment to their professional practice equal to that of their full-time colleagues (Anderson, 2008; Harris and Shelswell, 2005). In terms of teaching practice as an element of the **shared repertoire** of the CoP (as discussed in Chapter 4), the part-time tutor is no different from the full-time lecturer in terms of how they contribute to that practice: the stuff of teaching done by a part-time tutor is the same as the stuff done by a full-timer. From this point of view, our new tutor, fresh from her university studies and a newcomer to the CoP of the English course, is engaged in **legitimate**

peripheral practice – learning about the practice of the CoP on an **inbound trajectory**, whilst her students are learning about the CoP on **peripheral** and **outbound trajectories**. However, her part-time status prevents her from a trajectory towards full participation and so she decides to boost her CV by gaining a teaching qualification.

A PGCE (PCET) student

CoP theory has been widely uses to explore and describe both initial and continuing teacher education across a variety of sectors, including technical and vocational education, and could easily form the focus of an entire book (Chan, 2012; Goh, 2013, 2015; Tummons, 2008; Viskovic, 2005, 2006). For our part-time tutor, her time spent within the Community of Teacher Education Practice can be characterised firstly as a sustained period occupying a **peripheral, outbound trajectory**. She is travelling through this CoP in order to participate in enough of the practice of the community to allow her to acquire the ways of knowing and capacities that she needs to be seen by the wider world as a qualified teacher – so her participation is **peripheral** (she does not want to become a teacher educator – an old-timer within the CoP) and **outbound** (her participation is fixed in duration).

Meantime, our tutor also provides a further example of **multimembership** (as discussed above), as her participation in the Teacher Education CoP runs alongside her participation in the English CoP. In fact, the relationship between these two aspects of her multimembership illustrates another aspect of CoP theory at work. In order to join the Teacher Education CoP, she had to demonstrate that she had satisfied the *entry requirements* for the course, of which there were two. First, she had to provide a copy of any prior qualifications at level three or higher that demonstrated that she was qualified in her subject specialism – for this, she supplied a copy of her degree certificate. Second, she had to provide details of her contracted teaching hours, because she had chosen the *in-service* Teacher Education pathway – only open to those already employed at least part-time in a further or adult education setting (this might include trainers based in industry as well as in educational settings). From a CoP perspective, being an admissions tutor is a form of **brokerage** to allow people – potential students – to **cross the border** into the CoP, so long as they satisfy the gatekeeping requirements of both qualifications and experience.

Other forms of **boundary crossing** are easy to find within the Teacher Education CoP – indeed, it can be argued that without boundary crossings, the community would not be able to function in the way that it has been established over time. But first, a note of clarification: Our tutor – now also a PGCE student – does not cross boundaries between two CoPs (Teacher Education, and English); instead, she is at a point or **nexus of multimembership**. Boundary crossings are different and involve cross-CoP traffic that does not lead to permanent settlement. For example: for one of her PGCE/CertEd assignments (more on this in the following chapter) she has to be observed whilst teaching one of her student groups. Across the course as a whole, some of these observations will be done by a member of the PGCE/CertEd team, and others will be done by a subject-specialist *mentor* who is not normally part of the PGCE/CertEd CoP, but part of the English CoP where our tutor also works. After the observation, the observer writes their report, and our tutor – as a student, this time – writes a reflective commentary. These documents, together with her scheme of work, resources, and so forth, all go into her assignment portfolio.

So, what we have here is a series of **border crossings** with our tutor/student's **multimembership** at the centre. The PGCE/CertEd observers travel in one direction, carrying the observation forms with them. The completed observation forms then go back to where they belong – the Teacher Education CoP – inside our tutor/student's portfolio. At the same time, the scheme of work and teaching resources travel in the other direction. They stay as artefacts from the English CoP but are being borrowed or co-opted for a specific purpose within the Teacher Education CoP – as part of the portfolio – in just the same way as a qualification certificate is co-opted for a different specific purpose – to allow the holder of the qualification to gain admittance to a CoP in the first instance.

A CELTA student

As we read at the start of the chapter, our tutor wasn't able to get a full-time post even with her PGCE certificate (a not uncommon event, in fact) and so she decides to retrain as an ESOL specialist, choosing to do a part-time CELTA course that she can afford to do, and that fits in around her English teaching commitments. Being part of the CELTA CoP means that her CELTA assignments provide further examples of border crossings, familiar to her from her PGCE/CertEd. And there is a further level of complexity: thanks to her experiences of multimembership from both the PGCE/CertEd and English CoPs, some aspects of the CELTA CoP practice and repertoire are already familiar to her. Or, to put it another way, her **identity** as a result of her past and present multimembership allows her to bring aspects of the repertoires of other CoPs to work within the CELTA community. *Lesson planning* is a practice that she has acquired during her time as a part-time tutor, rehearsed during staff training days (which as an assiduous part-timer she still found the time to attend), and been taught about and assessed on during her PGCE/CertEd. The paperwork is different and the subject matter is of course now different as well, but the lesson planning practices of the two CoPs – PGCE/CertEd and CELTA – share much common ground: they are an example of **alignment** between the two communities (Wenger, 1998: 178–81).

A full-time ESOL college lecturer, with a course leadership role, and maintaining a small amount of evening-class teaching.

Finally, we meet our lecturer as she is today – as a full-time member of staff at the college, balancing teaching with course leadership, and now being asked to cover some BTEC Business classes. As a full-time member of staff with a course leadership role, her trajectory within the ESOL community is that of the **inbound insider**. Her now-regular contact with the awarding body for the curriculum has started to open up new lines of communication with another CoP that is **aligned** to hers – the practices of the ESOL awarding body are self-evidently linked to the delivery of the ESOL programme in this (or any other) college. Verification and examination processes are conducted through several different kinds of **border crossing**, sometimes accompanied by **brokers** whilst at other times the documents that travel across borders – from awarding body to college and back again – are unaccompanied, and have to speak for themselves. Sometimes, other CoPs within the college have to get involved in the ESOL community, whether it is a CoP with an administrative function (admissions and registration, funding, assessment registration, and so forth) or with a pedagogical function (learning support). Within the constellation of CoPs that make up the college, our lecturer is a full participant in at least one (the ESOL CoP), a more peripheral participant in another (the English evening classes), a broker for some aspects of the ESOL CoP when speaking with brokers from the awarding body, and a gatekeeper for other aspects, when dealing with admissions.

And after all of this, she now finds herself at the boundary – or perhaps the periphery? – of the BTEC Business CoP. This is another community that is part of the college constellation, with some alignment to the other CoPs that she is part of: a small amount of the syllabus is familiar, and many of the administrative processes, both internal and external, are similar. In addition, she has already noticed some recognisable patterns of both **mutual engagement** (how things get done) and **shared repertoire** (the resources and tools used to get things done). It is the **joint enterprise** – the thing that the CoP is about – that is quite distinct. She had not planned on joining this community, but political pressures from elsewhere in the constellation have made it necessary for her to do so, even if only on a **peripheral** trajectory. She is very much a newcomer to this CoP, but her **identity**, formed over time through differing levels of membership in other CoPs that are about the stuff of further and adult education in all kinds of ways, will help her navigate this BTEC Business CoP – so long as she can find the hours in the day to do both the **reconciliation** work required, and the reading that underpins the practice of this new – to her – community.

Some conclusions

Moving across and between different Communities of Practice is, I suggest, typical of pretty much everyone who works in further and adult education. Sometimes, these moments of boundary crossing can be difficult to accomplish and hard to be reconciled with – as in the case of the new vocational tutors who were the focus of Selena Chan's research, discussed above. At other times, boundary crossing is something that, as individual community members, we set out to do – as in the case of our fictional college lecturer, whose career story illustrated the conceptual themes of this chapter. However it happens and for whatever reason, this cross-community traffic is a common, even necessary, aspect of the practice of any community. CoPs need new people and new artefacts, sometimes to absorb and call their own, sometimes to provide an injection of novelty, note of concern, or simply friendly conversation. It would need a highly complex diagram to map out all of the CoPs in just one college, let alone a national sector. But what we can do is trace the constellations of CoPs that we are enrolled in as teachers and as vocational/professional experts, in order to make sense of the different directions that we have to travel and the different ways in which we are sometimes pushed.

References

Anderson, V. (2008) Communities of practice and part-time lecturers: opportunities and challenges in higher education. In Kimble, C., Hildreth, P., and Bourdon, I. (eds) *Communities of Practice I: creating learning environments for educators*. Charlotte, NC: IAP. 83–102.

Belfiore, M., Defoe, T., Folinsbee, S., Hunter, J., and Jackson, N. (2004) *Reading Work: Literacies in the New Workplace*. New Jersey: Lawrence Erlbaum Associates.

Boud, D. and Middleton, H. (2003) Learning from others at work: communities of practice and informal learning. *Journal of Workplace Learning* 15 (5) 194–202. doi:10.1108/13665620310483895.

Chan, S. (2012) Perspectives of new trades tutors: boundary crossing between vocational identities. *Asia-Pacific Journal of Teacher Education* 40 (4) 409–421. doi:10.1080/1359866X.2012.724656.

Goh, A.Y.S. (2013) The significance of social relationships in learning to become a vocational and technical education teacher. *Studies in Continuing Education* 35 (3) 366–378. doi:10.1080/0158037X.2013.770390.

Goh, A.Y.S. (2015) An individual learning journey: learning as becoming a vocational teacher. *International Journal of Lifelong Education* 34 (6) 680–695. doi:10.1080/02601370.2015.1096311.

Harris S. and Shelswell, N. (2005) Moving beyond communities of practice in adult basic education. In Barton, D. and Tusting, K. (eds.) *Beyond Communities of Practice: Language, Power and Social Context*. Cambridge: Cambridge University Press. 158–179.

Herne, S. (2006) Communities of practice in art and design and museum and gallery education. *Pedagogy, Culture and Society* 14 (1) 1–17. DOI:doi:10.1080/14681360500487512.

Kamp, A. (2019) Post-compulsory education and training in Aotearoa New Zealand. In Tummons, J. (ed.) *PCET: learning and teaching in the post-compulsory sector*. London: Sage/Learning Matters. 248–262.

Lemke, J. (1997) Cognition, context and learning: a social semiotic perspective. In Kirshner, D. and Whitson, J. (eds.) *Situated Cognition: Social, Semiotic and Psychological Perspectives*. London: Lawrence Erlbaum. 37–56.

Star, S.L. and Griesemer, J. (1989) Institutional ecology, 'translations' and boundary objects: amateurs and professionals in Berkeley's museum of vertebrate zoology, 1907–39. *Social Studies of Science* 19 (3) 387–420. doi:10.1177%2F030631289019003001.

Tummons, J. (2008) Assessment, and the literacy practices of trainee PCET teachers. *International Journal of Educational Research* 47(3): 184–191. doi:10.1016/j.ijer.2008.01.006.

94   *Constellations, boundaries, and brokers*

Tummons, J. (2018) *Learning architectures in higher education: beyond communities of practice.* London: Bloomsbury.

Viskovic, A. (2005) 'Community of Practice' as a Framework for Supporting Tertiary Teachers' Informal Workplace Learning. *Journal of Vocational Education and Training* 57 (3) 389–410. doi:10.1080/13636820500200293.

Viskovic, A. (2006) Becoming a tertiary teacher: learning in communities of practice. *Higher Education Research and Development* 25 (4) 323–339. doi:10.1080/07294360600947285.

Wenger, E. (1998) *Communities of Practice: Learning, Meaning and Identity.* Cambridge: Cambridge University Press.

7 Assessment within a Community of Practice

Introduction

In this seventh chapter, I am going to explain how we can make sense of assessment as an aspect of the shared repertoire of any Community of Pedagogical Practice. From the point of view of the first incarnation of the theory, assessment is, arguably, antithetical to any CoP, symbolising as it does the characteristics of formal models of educational provision that Jean Lave, in particular, was committed to critiquing. However, the later ideas of Etienne Wenger provide a way through which we can interpose assessment as an aspect of the theory that, if we are careful, will maintain the integrity of the CoP framework whilst expanding somewhat on the model of the learning architecture that we have already explored.

Qualifications, certificates, and credentials

There are several aspects of formal educational provision that, irrespective of the age range of the students or learners, are visible to the rest of the world, and that in their own different ways help to mark out or signify the **boundaries** of Communities of Educational Practice. The actual places – the buildings, or areas of buildings – where educational provision happens are one of these. The uniforms and/or lanyards that students as well as staff wear are another. A third marker or symbol of these CoPs is a qualifications certificate – the all-important piece of paper that the student can take with them when they leave the community. Certificates do several things: they carry messages about what that individual has done within the CoP in question; they persuade employers or admissions tutors to allow the bearer of the certificate to pass across the boundaries that they are responsible for maintaining; and they allow the various CoPs that helped to bring them into existence as physical documents – educational institutions, sites of employment (for placement learning, day release, and so forth), and awarding bodies – to demonstrate these achievements to outsiders in order to secure funding, establish new **brokerage** arrangements, as well as sustain their own practices.

So far so good, except that we now need to do a little more theoretical groundwork before we can make sense of all of this. Describing a certificate as

DOI: 10.4324/9781003252566-7

an example of an artefact within a CoP is straightforward, and the idea that it can travel about as a **boundary object** (as discussed in the preceding chapter) follows on from this – and we shall describe these processes in more detail below. But before we can discuss how a certificate travels across a constellation of communities, we need to work out how the certificate actually came into existence in the first place. In order to do this, we need to think about the assessment processes that all come together and lead up to the generating of a certificate. But we can't do that without first thinking about assessment as an aspect of pedagogical practice – the work of the trainer and teacher – that slots into a CoP. This will require some careful thinking. In Chapter 4, we found a way to resolve the *pedagogy problem* within CoP theory – a way to take a model of instruction for formal educational provision, and reconcile it to a theoretical framework that has its roots in informal, non-institutional settings. What we now have to do is to solve a related problem – let's call it the *assessment problem* – in order to find ways to fit assessment into the **joint enterprise** of a formal educational CoP.

Our first step is to think about social practice accounts of assessment – research and writing that does not explore assessment from the point of view of psychology or psychometrics, cognitive load or learning gain (all of which are open to critique) but in terms of the everyday stuff that people do in order for assessment to happen. In doing so, we will be able to see how a social practice theory of assessment is a further example of a *theoretical plug-in* (as discussed in Chapter 3) that can fit into a CoP quite neatly. The second step will require us to come at the *assessment problem* from the other direction, as it were, to return to CoP theory and to use it as the basis for a 'native' solution to the problem. Once we have taken these two steps, all of the more familiar aspects of assessment theory that are found in CertEd/PGCE syllabuses, professional standards, awarding body handbooks, and so forth – in particular *validity* and *reliability* – will fall into place within the CoP framework. And finally, with one further element of CoP theory added from Wenger (1998), we will be able to explain how certificates come into being and account for the work that they do.

Assessment as a social practice

Thinking about assessment as a social practice means focussing on those different things that people do – this might be apprentices or instructors, internal verifiers or external examiners – that are about or related to the doing of assessment in a broad sense. For example, when thinking about portfolio-based assessment – a common format form assessment across many vocational curricula (Ecclestone et al., 2010) – we might think about the ways in which any NVQ candidate might go about the work of collecting together the evidence that they need to demonstrate competence in any one aspect of the curriculum. For any assessment, not just for the purposes of an NVQ, one important quality is *validity* – does the assessment actually assess the content that it sets out to assess, and does the assessment process provide a justification for the ways in which the assessment results will be used? Assessment theory, including validity, is a key topic within teacher education programmes, and additional guidance can invariably be found on the websites of awarding bodies. A statistician might measure assessment validity through the analysis of test results in order to establish the *validity coefficient* of the test. If we are going to think about assessment validity from a social practice standpoint, however, we would not look to measure validity, but to account for how we arrived at a definition of validity in the first place and then, more importantly, how different teachers and trainers make sense of assessment validity and then use their understanding of validity to shape their assessment practices. Happily, assessment theory and practice within further and adult education is one area of inquiry that is well represented within the research literature, and an increasing number of researchers have begun to adopt a social practice perspective. Some have used Communities of Practice theory, others have used different social theories that nonetheless, if we are cautious, can help us in our present inquiry because of the compatibilities that exist between different approaches (as discussed in Chapter 3). From this research perspective, discussions of issues such as formative and summative assessment or assessment validity take on a rather different tone.

Interlude: exploring assessment theory from a social practice perspective

In Chapter 5, I introduced the *Transforming Learning Cultures in Further Education* project. That project did not look directly at assessment, but a later research project led by Kathryn Ecclestone that drew on the same learning cultures approach explored formative assessment across a range of different sites, including part-time ESOL provision and a full-time BTEC Diploma in Public Services in a large FE college, and business studies for 14–16 year-old students on a 'link' course at a community college (Ecclestone et al., 2010). Ecclestone and her colleagues were interested in, amongst other things, the blurring of the boundaries between *formative* assessment ('assessment for learning') and *summative* assessment ('assessment of learning'). Through their research, they found variation between the ways that these two modes of assessment were both understood and practiced in different sites. However, this variation was due not only to the different requirements of different curricula, but also the different cultures of different sites. In some settings, external pressures to maintain or improve assignment results were more likely to have been experienced by practitioners who would then react to these pressures in different ways. It is only through examining the everyday work of practitioners that these findings can be brought to light.

Assessment *validity* is another key theory. There are several different elements of assessment validity, and one of particular salience to the present discussion is the concept of assessment *authenticity*. In a comparative case study conducted by Crisp and Novaković (2009), assessment materials from a Business Administration NVQ – worksheets, portfolios, activity plans, and so forth – from five different sites were collected together and then analysed by a group of 15 examiners, moderators, and tutors. After this, follow-up interviews were conducted at four of the colleges. Two key findings came from the research. First, they found that even though the tasks required of candidates at the five colleges were all fairly similar (the tutors who designed the tasks were all working within the same NVQ framework), there was variation between centres in terms of how *demanding* the tasks were – how complex the tasks were, and how many and what types of resources were required. Second, they found considerable variety in *authenticity* between sites, most commonly related to the balance between candidates' access to real work experience on the one hand, and the use of simulation in order to generate assessment tasks on the other, with consequent implications for assessment validity.

In the broadest sense, therefore, social practice accounts of assessment help us to foreground the kinds of stories that get lost sight of when we read the reports written by internal verifiers, or when we turn the pages of a portfolio of evidence. Quality assurance processes describe assessment work in ways that suggest that everything is sufficient, valid, and reliable: results are checked two or even three times; the work of different assessors has been moderated according to awarding body criteria; there is a robust alignment between curriculum requirements and assessment activity. Social practice research tells us something rather different, however. It informs us that assessment is sufficient, valid, and reliable *enough* but that the processes that get us to this point are far from straightforward, and will never be complete: an assessment task is never 'completely' valid or 'perfectly' reliable.

Assessment as a social practice involves not only the busy work of marking projects, form filling, helping students complete ILPs, organising placements, and helping our colleagues. It also entails an understanding of the wider implications of social and cultural factors such as ethnicity (Ball et al., 1998) or class or gender (Colley et al., 2003 – as discussed in Chapter 5) on how assessment gets done, of the effects of the family backgrounds of our trainees or apprentices on assessment, and of the ways in which management procedures (Crisp and Novaković, 2009 – as discussed above) and funding changes impact on classroom assessment practice. The actual instance of testing or examination, no matter how it is done, is only one small part of the broader work of assessment within further and adult education.

Having established that we can shift our point of view by thinking about assessment as a social practice, we are now in a position to bring things into even sharper focus, and describe assessment in terms of one specific social practice theory – Communities of Practice. We need to draw on some specific elements of CoP theory and map them to a theoretical understanding of assessment and to evaluate the ways in which CoP theory has already been used to make sense of assessment within further and adult education.

Assessment in a Community of Practice

In Chapter 4, we resolved the *pedagogy problem*, thinking of ways in which we can reconcile a mode of instruction with a theoretical framework for explaining learning in social contexts that resolutely rejected any such formal pedagogical practices and resources. Assessment, likewise, poses problems from the point of view of an unadulterated use of Lave and Wenger's theories. A formal practice of assessment, involving the judgements of teachers, the creation of procedures and materials, and the construction by learners of materials that have only been brought into being in the first place in order to complete the assessment task, is also incompatible with the ideas expressed in *Situated Learning* (Lave and Wenger, 1991). If you are busy generating stuff in order to demonstrate your capacity or competence, you are not actually engaged in the practice of the CoP – you are generating materials that are *about* the practice of the CoP. **Legitimate Peripheral Participation** is not a 'pedagogical strategy or a teaching technique' but a model of learning that happens 'no matter which educational form provides a context for learning, or whether there is *any* educational form at all' (Lave and Wenger, 1991: 40 – emphasis added). For Lave and Wenger, there are 'conflicts between learning to know and learning to display knowledge for evaluation' (ibid., 112): this is a profound rejection of formal assessment. Wenger's later addition to the theory, **Learning Architecture** (discussed in Chapter 4) provides us with a framework for pedagogy and for formal instruction, but still no clear statement as to how assessment might be part of this framework. Assuming that we all subscribe to the view that assessment of some kind is an unavoidable element of formal education and training across all sectors (although I acknowledge that there are some serious disagreements to this), it seems right to plug the gap and to think about those elements of CoP theory that might help us.

Just as the further and adult education sectors are underrepresented in the research literature, the exploration of assessment is a rarer topic still. Indeed, the first comprehensive cross-sector research into assessment and feedback practices was only completed 17 years ago, at the time of writing – a large-scale research project into different methods of assessment that, fortunately for our present discussion, made some use of social theory and CoP theory.

Interlude: The impact of different modes of assessment on achievement and progress in the learning and skills sector

This research was funded by the (now defunct) Learning and Skills Research Centre (LSRC), the City and Guilds Awarding Body, and the (also now defunct) University for Industry (UfI). Led by Harry Torrance, the research team collected together questionnaire responses from 260 people and interviewed 237 learners/ NVQ candidates and 95 assessors/teachers, from across nine different curriculum areas. In seeking to explore the extent to which assessment methods might directly affect progress and achievement, the research team found that they did not. What they did find was that students would shy away from courses that used assessment methods that they disliked, that tutors and lecturers provided much effective coaching and feedback, and that competence-based and criterion-based assessments were beneficial to learners generally. A further finding was the variability between sites in the application of national standards and their relationship to localised interpretations. Torrance et al. framed this in terms of 'localised communities of practice' (2005: 2). More specifically, they write that 'it is helpful to see the methods, tasks, arrangements and all practicalities of assessment as both what is written in "the rules" (reification) and what people actually do in a particular situation (participation) – and to appreciate how these are mutually dependent' (Torrance et al., 2005: 19). **Reification** and **participation** are two further key concepts from Wenger (1998) that we have yet to encounter, and I shall return to these shortly. What is important for now is the gap that Torrance et al. identify as coming in between what the guidelines say on the one hand, and what people actually do on the other. They locate this gap between two kinds of CoP that they label as vertical and horizontal (Torrance et al., 2005: 76). The vertical CoPs are those of the industrial practices, academic disciplines and awarding bodies, and so forth; and the horizontal CoPs are the local, geographically situated communities of assessors, tutors, learner, and apprentices. Distinguishing between these different CoPs makes sense although I do not agree with their horizontal/vertical division: industrial practice can be local, after all, and tutors and learners can be geographically distributed (especially when using information and communication technologies). Why not use the concepts of constellations and borders?

The linked concepts of **participation** and **reification** (Wenger, 1998: 55–62) are vital to any attempt to insert a theory of assessment into Communities of Practice, and therefore deserve a second outing (see our earlier discussion in Chapter 4). Participation is straightforward, and simply refers to the process of taking part in something. However, Wenger reserves the concept of participation for the *people* who are members of a CoP: an apprentice participates in the practice of the community, but the *tools* or *object* that they might use do not participate: they are used, employed, adjusted, or modified by the participants. Participation in practice is what allows our apprentice to engage in learning through **legitimate peripheral participation**, to grow and shift their **identities**, and so forth.

Reification is a much less common word. When we **reify** something we take something that is an abstract or mental thing and convert it into a physical one. For example: the notion of 'justice' is a philosophical and abstract thing – we can talk about it and argue about it, but we can't pick it up and move it around in our hands. But if we took some of those ideas about justice and used them to pass a law – a statute – then we would have generated a physical, concrete form – a **reification** – that we can indeed carry around, post online, send to people, table at meetings, and so forth. If we wanted to **reify** an abstract notion such as 'professionalism', we could generate a series of professional standards that would then be able to exist on a piece of paper or as a PDF document – just as the ETF Standards do. The decision to **reify** something makes that thing concrete and physical, but it does not follow that a reification lasts forever. The *Lifelong Learning UK* professional standards were an earlier reification of teacher professionalism, and the *Further Education National Training Organisation* standards were earlier still. They still exist insofar as you can find them on a website (although tracking down a PDF of the FEnto standards is surprisingly tricky) but they no longer get picked up and used except very occasionally by researchers, and then for a very different purpose than for which they were designed and reified in the first place.

Dealing with reifications is not straightforward, therefore. Firstly, we can see that it is not possible to capture perfectly the thing that we had as an abstract thing when we convert it into a concrete one. Discussions about professionalism – professional knowledge, ethics, codes of practice, professionalisation, and so forth – are hard to capture in one place. 'Justice' is a far-reaching concept that cannot be reduced to just one or even a number of statutes. Any reified form, therefore, is always *partial* – it only captures some of whatever it is that is being converted into a solid form. And secondly, we can see that once we have got a reified form, it does not follow that everyone will automatically use, read, or interpret it *in the same way*. Statutes are made, but are then disputed in law courts as meanings are worked out in practice. Professional frameworks such as the ETF standards can't please everyone all of the time: one of the standards asks teachers and trainers to 'maintain and update your knowledge of educational research to develop evidence-based practice' – but there are profound debates within universities, research offices, and examining bodies as to what educational research should or should not do, how evidence can be derived from research, whether all research generates findings that are generalisable, and so forth.

If reifications are less-than-perfect representations of more complicated mental or abstract topics and ideas, and are also less-than-perfect because they are capable of being misinterpreted or misread, then how should we make sense of what they do? The answer to this lies in thinking about the relationship between any reified thing, and the people who are going to use it in some way. The work that a reification can or might do can only be understood once we remember that we need at least one person to help with that work: a book cannot read itself; a tool cannot pick itself up; a PDF file cannot email itself. Reified objects *always* need some people to help them do what they do. Someone needs to pick up a book and turn the pages, open the PDF file on screen, pick up the tool, and apply it to the correct process. Some people may then disagree with or even ignore what they are reading, and move to something else; other people will discard the tool that they have selected and use a different one. Alternatively, someone might be so inspired by what they read that they change aspects of their practice, or use the tool in order to master a specific operational technique for the first time.

Simply put, the way in which we engage in practice within our communities rests on any number of reifications. Some of these will have been around for a long time and others will be new. We might create some of these and adjust or modify others. Some might be used frequently and others might get ignored, rendered obsolete, or left behind. Any kind of object or artefact within a CoP is a **reification** – something that started out as an idea and has now been made into a tangible, practical thing, and it is through our **participation** in practice that they are activated – brought into use – or deactivated – put to one side. Participation and reification, therefore, always go together.

The participation and reification of assessment practices

Assessment and feedback practices are as varied as the curricula that a college can offer. Some courses are assessed predominantly through practical work – either in the workplace or in a simulated environment, depending on whether the course is work-based or work-related. This might be observed by a suitably qualified assessor (scheme documentation invariably provides guidelines in terms of occupational competence/expertise), might be photographed to generate evidence for a portfolio, or might be the subject of a witness testimony. Courses ranging from trowel occupations to play-work rely on students engaging in practice and then capturing elements of that practice in a format that will allow for all of the necessary steps in the assessment process to happen. Other courses will be assessed through assignments that are set by the awarding body and then either internally or (less frequently) externally assessed or graded. Some courses are assessed through project work and others through compiling portfolios. Some course assessments require reports from work placements, and others ask for employers or workplace assessors as well as college-based staff to make assessment decisions and/or contribute evidence of achievement. My guess is that for the people who are reading this book, the stuff of assessment and feedback is familiar. This might be in the many different kinds of formative and summative tasks that students are asked to complete and the different kinds of ways in which we give feedback. Or it might be in the ways in which we, as teachers and trainers, have to gather assessment materials up for the purposes of internal moderation and external verification as part of the quality assurance processes that help establish consistency and reliability between assessors and across centres.

So let us take these familiar assessment objects and processes – or, better, **artefacts** – and think about them in terms of **participation** and **reification** in order to gain some new insights. The research by Torrance et al. does include references to reification and participation (2005: 18–19), but they limit their inquiry to thinking about the differences between the guidelines provided by awarding bodies (as reification) and the day-to-day stuff that lecturers and assessors do on the ground, at local level (as participation). Torrance et al. are right to highlight the gap between the awarding body documentation on the one hand and how they are locally interpreted on the other – but there is more that we can do with the concepts. For example: we know, thanks to CoP theory, that participation and reification always go together. Our college lecturers' participation is shaped by the awarding body reifications, which they interpret in particular ways during their ongoing participation – it's a circular, give-and-take process. But assessment guidelines are only one example of a reified artefact that we might find in and amongst all of the stuff of assessment. The other kinds of assessment documents that I referred to above – witness statements, photographs, projects, external verifier reports, and all the rest – are *also* reifications that have come into being in physical forms as a result of the participation of the different apprentices, students, verifiers, and so on, all going about their work.

Interlude: the many reified texts of vocational assessment

It's time to introduce another large-scale research project that explored aspects of learning within the FE sector: the *Literacies for Learning in Further Education* project (LFLFE), a three-and-a-half year project based on collaboration between two universities and four FE colleges (Ivanič et al., 2009). The project rested on a social practice theory of literacy. In Chapter 3, I discussed the research by Sligo et al. (2019) that explored the differing literacy requirements of vocational workplaces and educational institutions, and in Chapter 5 I discussed the possibility of using *literacy studies* as a theoretical plug-in for CoPs. The LFLFE project occupies the same ground. One of the many in-depth descriptions of learner practice included in the book detailed the many different *text-based* activities observed during a typical day in a college training restaurant (Ivanič et al., 2009: 85–87), which included (these are by no means all of them):

- Checking names in the booking diary.
- Checking stock.
- Talking through the menu with the catering staff and tutors.
- Practising taking food and/or drinks orders.
- Actually taking food and/or drinks orders.
- Completing entries in logbooks against different course criteria, which the tutor would then check.
- Reading booklets produced by the tutor, covering underpinning knowledge requirements.
- Writing answers to knowledge questions in the booklets that would later be copied into the logbooks.

This busy day in the training restaurant is typical of lots of different technical and vocational settings in that the trainees are here doing a mixture of things. They are engaged in tasks that are work-based (checking stock, taking food orders), work-related (practising taking food orders), and then more specifically assessment-related (completing their logbooks, writing answers in the booklets). It's impossible to put 'taking a food order' into a portfolio, and so a reification is needed that in some way converts the physical, embodied practice of taking a food order into a physical document that can be slotted into a portfolio – this is what happens when the individual candidate *evidences* their work. Similarly, a trainee on the trowel occupations NVQ that we encountered earlier obviously cannot put a fireplace or a brick arch into a portfolio – but a photograph of the fireplace and a report from a workplace assessor – both reifications – take the place of the actual bricks, as it were. Tutors and students all generate reifications of different kinds. The booklets produced by the tutors at the training restaurant, which act as a 'go-between' with the students on one side and the official awarding body documents on the other, are a reification. The written answers of the student are a reification. And, just as importantly, the workplace itself is a site where reifications are generated – menus, bookings, invoices, and stock orders. Assessment is an aspect of the practice of the community that both requires *and* generates reifications.

Portfolios reify the progress and actions of the learners: all of their learning – their **practice** – gets converted into a portfolio (or an essay for an academic curriculum – the principle remains the same). Feedback forms, mark sheets, and so forth reify the assessment decisions and feedback from the tutors. Moderation and verification forms reify the quality assurance processes that all of the assessment decisions made by tutors and work done by learners have to be measured against, to ensure consistency. These reifications travel in a number of different directions across the **constellations** of communities that make up the sector as a whole. Student portfolios (in the broadest sense) spend most of their time at first travelling from colleges to workplaces and/or sites where work-related simulations are being provided. Later, they might travel across college for internal moderation, or between colleges for a cross-centre event, in just the same way that course documentation travels from awarding bodies to colleges – across different **borders** between CoPs. Candidates may well wish to keep their portfolios when they leave their CoPs (remember – students are only ever on a **peripheral** and **outbound** trajectory, as discussed in Chapter 2), but the artefacts reified by teachers and moderators will always stay within the constellation. But a portfolio by itself is not much help for the candidate in obtaining a job. One more transformation or reification is needed in order for the assessment process to come to a close – certification.

Qualifications and certificates – artefacts of accomplishment

The most common way through which we might persuade somebody – an admissions tutor, a potential employer – that we are competent, qualified, or otherwise demonstrably in possession of a particular body of competencies and skills, or of knowledge, is to provide copies of our qualifications. The receipt of a certificate at the (successful) end of a course or programme of study provides us with a way to show anybody – assuming they know how to read and/or interpret it – a document that 'proves' what we can do or know. Once we have left the CoP that we had previously been part of on a peripheral and outbound trajectory, the certificate(s) that we have received and taken with us become the most straightforward way for others to see what we have learned, or – more correctly – to see that we have learned something. The certificate is a stand-in, a proxy for our completed learning trajectory. All of our time within the CoP in question – our engagement with the shared repertoire, our learning about the discourses of the community, our participation and reification – is all wrapped up in the certificate. As a consequence of our learning during our time in that CoP, our capacities and attributes – our **identities** – have changed and been changed, but these are sometimes hard to see or to verbalise. A certificate is a convenient, inexpensive (by itself – they are usually just pieces of paper, after all) and portable reification, an artefact that sums up our accomplishments. More precisely, a certificate is a **boundary object**. It is generated – reified – within a specific CoP, but does not form part of the shared repertoire of that CoP. It is designed and manufactured for one specific purpose – to carry a specific message to the wider world concerning the person who holds it, namely that they have successfully completed a particular programme of study. But how can the reader of the certificate be confident in the messages that it conveys?

Assessment theory and Communities of Practice

Assessment theory is a well-established component of initial teacher education curricula and of continuing professional development. This is hardly surprising, mindful of the central role that assessment plays across the further and adult education sector as a whole. Students want to know that they are being assessed fairly, tutors want to know that their assessment decisions are being made for the right reasons, employers want to know that assessments provide reliable indicators of competence and capability, and funding agencies want to know that assessment processes are robust and efficient. Assessment is, arguably, one of the most visible aspects of the practice of the sector – of the practice of the constellations that make up the sector. Confidence – of any and all of these stakeholders – is established through the maintenance of assessment quality, and this in turn relies on assessments of every mode (portfolio, project, assignment, simulation) being both *valid* and *reliable*.

Validity and reliability have already been discussed in this chapter and are well established within teacher education literature, and there is not enough room here to explore in full the many debates that surround these constructs. For now, it is sufficient to remember that for an assessment to be a valid assessment, it must assess the actual body of knowledge of skill that the course or programme of study set out to deliver, provide adequate coverage of the content of the course, be appropriate to the subjects being studied and assessed, and be able to predict the future performance of the student. For an assessment to be reliable, it must display consistency, ensuring that personal or environmental factors do not affect the assessment process: irrespective of who the assessor is and where and when the assessment takes place, the outcome must be the same. A further element of assessment validity that is of particular importance to technical and vocational education and training (although it pertains also to academic programmes) is *authenticity*. Earlier, I referred to the research by Crisp and Novaković (2009) who wanted to explore authenticity in assessment across different sites. Within CoP theory, however, authenticity takes on a slightly different role that impacts on not only assessment, but on learning as well.

We already know (from our discussion in Chapter 2) that apprenticeship learning through legitimate peripheral participation requires opportunities for engaging in the authentic practices of the community. We also know that we can access authentic experience through **brokering** work (discussed in Chapter 3). We know that a learning architecture requires authenticity in all of its resources if it is to generate opportunities for meaningful learning (discussed in Chapter 4), and, finally, we know that for some commentators, Lave and

Wenger's emphasis on authenticity forms part of their critique of formal educational institutions (discussed in Chapter 5). Within a learning architecture, Wenger argues that teachers, as one of the structuring resources, need to embody 'lived authenticity' and not let this be overshadowed by their 'pedagogical and institutional functions' (Wenger, 1998: 276) – a relationship between subject specialism and pedagogical knowledge that is captured in the notion of *dual professionalism*. Authenticity, within a CoP perspective, is the single most important element of assessment validity. It is not restricted to the embodied expertise and identities of teachers and trainers. It relates also to the sites, tools, and resources for learning, and to the tasks that students and apprentices are asked to complete.

Validity as authenticity is characteristic of, or – better – a necessary element of, assessment within a CoP, but we still need to make sense of reliability as well, not least as the relationship between validity and reliability is a frequent topic for discussion within assessment theory. These conversations usually proceed along the lines of 'if validity goes up, then reliability goes down, and vice versa' and so a balance has to be struck between the two. However, within a CoP, there is no correlation between validity and reliability, except insofar as they both rest on authenticity. It is through the lived authenticity of the teacher or trainer, as a more experienced, longer-standing member of the CoP, that legitimacy as an assessor or examiner is established. Their identity as 'old-timers' is an educational resource (Wenger, 1998: 277) in just the same way as their expertise, engagement, and practice are resources. Lave and Wenger may well have rejected any notions of evaluation within a CoP as being an inauthentic representation forced on the learner by any formalised curriculum within an institution (1991: 112), but if we are to accept the apprenticeship metaphor that is at the heart of their work, then at some point it must surely be the case that the more experienced member of the community needs to check in on the work done by a newcomer, to make sure that the work that the newcomer is doing is aligned to the **joint enterprise** of the community, is discussed, practiced, queried, and acknowledged through the **mutual engagement** of the community, and draws – in an appropriate and meaningful way – on the **shared repertoire** of the community.

Expertise and experience provides reliability in assessment, therefore. But there are two strands to this. The first is the expertise that pertains to the authentic practice of the vocation or craft – in plumbing, in media make-up application, in web design – and the second pertains to the practice of assessment as a pedagogical function – the understanding of the criteria, the use of the feedback forms, the difference between 'pass' and 'merit' level work on a BTEC award. This second strand is equally authentic, because it captures aspects of the authentic practice of being a teacher or trainer. The expertise in the craft – the specialist knowledge and competence of the community – is a resource to be accessed by students, a form of shared repertoire that students will participate in on a peripheral basis. The expertise in the practice of assessment is only for the fullest members of the community – the teachers and trainers – to employ in full: for the students, this is an element of the shared repertoire that they only *very* peripherally engage with. For the students, knowledge of assessment practice within the community is restricted, necessarily, to what they need to do: the tasks, the portfolio bundling, the hand-in dates, and so forth. For the teachers, knowledge of assessment practice is as important as knowledge of their specialism because both of these bodies of knowledge are elements of shared repertoire.

Interlude: a theoretical account of assessment within Communities of Practice

Of the relatively small number of academic papers or chapters that have explored assessment from a CoP perspective, only a few embrace the theoretical challenges posed by what I have termed the *assessment problem*. One of these is a paper published 20 years ago by Thomas Rømer, in which he addresses head-on the challenge to assessment theory and practice posed by a theory of situated learning within Communities of Practice. From the starting point expressed by Lave and Wenger that it is impossible to demonstrate any kind of knowledge (whether or not this is for the purpose of evaluation) outside the CoP in question, he draws on Wenger's notion of a CoP being, amongst other things, a 'regime of competence' (Wenger, 1998: 137), where competence is widely interpreted as being 'the distinctions that are given credit by the community' (Rømer, 2002: 238). He concludes: 'the condition for assessment and evaluation in the traditional interpretation of full participation is the assessor's knowledge of, and ability to relate to, the canonical texts of a tradition and his (sic) general integration in a community' (Rømer, 2002: 238).

But the notion of canonical texts implies a more complete coverage of a craft or skill than many curricula have room for: for practical reasons, a tradition – irrespective of the subject matter – needs to be parcelled up or reified so that it can slot into the social and organisational structures of formal education. With this refinement, we can see how Rømer's conclusion allows assessment to be slotted into a CoP, with the experience and expertise – the authenticity – of the assessor as a necessary precondition.

Pulling it all together: authentic reifications of learning

Finally, we are in a position to make sense of our certificates and qualifications, of how they came to be, and what they do:

1 A student joins a CoP as a legitimate, peripheral participant, following a peripheral and outbound trajectory.
2 They meet their tutor, a full participant, following an insider trajectory.
3 Over time, the student completes a series of tasks that pertain to the practices of the community, that are characterised by authenticity and, as such, are valid. Some of these tasks remain in the form that the student has completed them in (such as written project work). Others need to be

reworked or represented as text-based reifications. Some of these will be done by other people (such as witness statements or photographs) and some of these will be done by the student (such as a learning log or reflective journal) – all depending on the nature of the curriculum. They all capture elements of that student's community participation.

4 The work done for these tasks is assessed by the tutor who, thanks to their expertise and experience and their position as a full member – their authenticity of identity – provides a judgement that is reliable.

5 The tutor, drawing on a different aspect of their expertise, fulfils the requirements of the CoP in terms of formal recording of the tasks that the student has successfully completed. Feedback forms and so forth reify the judgements that they have made.

6 The reified forms of both the assessed work and the assessment judgements now are brought together so that representatives of other CoPs within the same constellation – verifiers and moderators – can oversee the processes that have been followed.

7 The representative of the relevant awarding body CoP in the constellation tells the tutor and the student that the assessment decisions that have been made have satisfied both themselves and any other CoP elsewhere in the constellation that has a legitimate interest, such as a professional body.

8 The student receives their certificate – a boundary object that they can carry across boundaries, and that works – that is to say, it carries messages about achievement and progress – outside the CoP where the student engaged in the practices that led to the eventual reification of that same certificate, and that they are now about to leave.

Some conclusions

What is assessment? It is an aspect of the shared repertoire of any Community of Pedagogic Practice within the constellation of CoPs that make up the further and adult education sector. It is a form of participation that involves different members of the community in different ways, depending on whereabouts in the community they are positioned. For full members – tutors and lecturers, assessors and mentors – assessment is an aspect of practice that they shape to some degree (mindful of the influences of external CoPs such as awarding bodies and professional organisations) before participation. The trajectory of the full members is such that their direction of travel towards assessment is in a different direction to that of the peripheral members – students, trainees, apprentices. For the students, the doing of assessment involves their increasingly full participation in the practice of the community, recorded and reified where necessary in assignments, portfolios, and the like. For the teachers, the doing of assessment involves their assumptive judgements about the merits and qualities of the work done by the students as newcomers, recorded in feedback forms, examiners' reports, and so forth. Assessment is an aspect of practice that is bound up in texts, that rests on the expertise of the teachers and the efforts of the students, and is rendered both valid and reliable through the practices of the teachers, the tasks that the students are asked to complete, the shared repertoire that both teachers and students work with: the authenticity of participation.

References

Ball, S., Maguire, M. and Macrae, S. (1998) 'Race', space and the further education market place. *Race Ethnicity and Education* 1 (2) 171–189. doi:10.1080/1361332980010203.

Colley, H., James, D., Diment, K., and Tedder, M. (2003) Learning as becoming in vocational education and training: class, gender and the role of vocational habitus. *Journal of Vocational Education and Training* 55 (4) 471–498. doi:10.1080/13636820300200240.

Crisp, V. and Novaković, N. (2009) Are all assessments equal? The comparability of demands of college-based assessments in a vocationally related qualification. *Research in Post-Compulsory Education* 14 (1) 1–18. doi:10.1080/13596740902717366.

Ecclestone, K., Davies, J., Derrick, J. and Gawn, J. (2010) *Transforming Formative Assessment in Lifelong Learning.* Maidenhead: McGraw-Hill.

Ivanič, R., Edwards, R., Barton, D., Martin-Jones, M., Fowler, Z., Hughes, B., Mannion, G., Miller, K., Satchwell, C., and Smith, J. (2009) *Improving learning in college: rethinking literacies across the curriculum.* London: Routledge.

Lave, J. and Wenger, E. (1991) *Situated Learning: Legitimate Peripheral Participation.* Cambridge: Cambridge University Press.

Rømer, T.A. (2002) Situated learning and assessment. *Assessment and Evaluation in Higher Education* 27 (3) 233–241. doi:10.1080/02602930220138598.

Torrance, H., Colley, H., Garratt, D., Jarvis, J., Piper, H., Ecclestone, K., and James, D. (2005) *The impact of different modes of assessment on achievement and progress in the learning and skills sector.* London: Learning and Skills Research Centre.

Wenger, E. (1998) *Communities of Practice: Learning, Meaning and Identity.* Cambridge: Cambridge University Press.

8 Communities of Practice

Opportunities and challenges for the further and adult education sectors

Introduction

In this final chapter I reflect on the broader nature of ongoing professional learning and development that is found within any profession, and apply these reflections to a consideration of the further and adult education sector. With all of the necessary conceptual building blocks having been patiently explained and put into their places, it is now, at last, time to explain the consequences for the sector of looking back at itself through lenses tinted by communities of practice theory.

Reflections on a lecture

A few days ago, at the time of writing, I was giving an invited talk to a group of lecturers and managers who worked at several colleges from across the North of England. What started as a conversation about continuing or continuous (both words are in use, but there is little meaningful difference) professional development (CPD) led to a further conversation about joint practice development (JPD) and then to Communities of Practice (CoP). From briefly outlining some key themes behind these three acronyms there soon followed a broader dialogue concerning the ownership of professional learning, the professional standards of the Education and Training Foundation and the different natures of subject-specific knowledge and pedagogical knowledge. For some, working in large departments, collaborations across colleges generated opportunities for new subject-specific networking; for others, working on smaller areas of provision, sometimes by themselves, such collaborations provided their only means of accessing meaningful opportunities to develop their practice alongside colleagues who shared their vocational or professional backgrounds as well as their pedagogical interests or concerns. For some, the idea of the Community of Practice was a relatively new one; for others, it was something that they had already come across and started to put to use.

It is always difficult to maintain a balance between a research-informed theoretical framework that exists at the level of academic discussion and writing on the one hand, and at the level of application to practice on the other. As a

DOI: 10.4324/9781003252566-8

practitioner, theory is arguably most compelling when it can be seen to directly inform an aspect of pedagogic practice. Assessment and feedback provide a good example of this. The ground-breaking work into *Assessment for Learning* done by Black and Wiliam, and first published over 20 years ago, has now become a well-established aspect of professional learning for teachers across all sectors. For many practitioners, the short booklet *Inside the Black Box: raising standards through classroom assessment* remains essential reading (Black and Wiliam, 1998a). Black and Wiliam were not the first people to make the distinction between formative and summative assessment, but they were among the first to build a compelling argument for the adoption of new approaches to classroom assessment based on the findings generated through research. They evaluated over 580 different chapters, articles, and so forth, and based their final review of the research evidence on 250 of these. This final review was published as an academic paper (Black and Wiliam, 1998b). *Inside the Black Box* is short, snappy, and more practical, containing a body of ideas that is waiting to be applied. There is a separate debate to be had about the effectiveness (whatever that might actually mean) or otherwise of Black and Wiliam's research, but the important point for now is that it was presented in what we might describe as a 'practitioner-friendly' format derived from a more extensive research project – a straightforward example of the findings of a research project being distilled for wider usage.

Now imagine that we have swapped Assessment for Learning with Communities of Practice. CoP theories have also been distilled and reduced in scale and complexity over time but unlike assessment for learning, the distillation of CoP theory has been accompanied by, and perhaps has caused, a series of over-simplifications. In part, this process was initiated by Wenger himself, who, a few years after the publication of *Communities of Practice*, went on to co-author a further volume that adopted a more applied approach (Wenger et al., 2002), reworking CoP theory for a business and management context and 'offering advice on the fostering of communities of practice in ways which improve economic competitiveness' (Barton and Tusting, 2005: 5). More generally, as the key concepts of CoP theory have been discussed, sometimes dissected, added to, and very occasionally strongly contradicted, it has also found itself more widely applied than critiqued, losing analytical potential in favour of becoming a formula for uncritical adoption (Hughes, 2007; Lea, 2005).

The teachers and trainers with whom I was speaking the other day were willing to actively engage with the detail of CoP theory as well as the broader notion of the community as an environment for sharing knowledge and practice – and many had already begun to do so in their own colleges, and with partners at neighbouring institutions. As members of a collection of colleges involved in one of the *Further Education Development Grant Pilot* (FEDGP) schemes funded by the Department for Education, they were already engaged in a research-informed project that, alongside the other initiatives within the FEDGP, sought to enhance the FE teaching workforce in a number of ways through a collaborative and (most importantly) sector-led approach to professional capacity building and development. (This pilot phase is currently drawing to a close.) Through focussing on themes including better induction and support for newly qualified and inexperienced teachers, developing online and blended pedagogies, and (of particular interest to the overarching line of argument presented in this book) enhancing subject-specific professional development and adopting evidence-based approaches, the FEDGP schemes are contributing to a lively conversation within the sector and not just about the sector.

This collaborative and sector-led approach, wrapped up as it is with a strong sense of ownership, chimes with the work done by the Education and Training Foundation (ETF) in encouraging ongoing professional learning and development. If we accept the conclusions drawn by, amongst others, Michael Eraut in his landmark study *Developing Professional Knowledge and Competence* (1994), then we agree that any professional qualification can only really be understood as a threshold qualification. That is to say, a professional qualification, often endorsed by a professional body, can be seen as demonstrating that the holder of that qualification has, through their study, gained sufficient knowledge, competence, ethical commitment and so forth to be allowed to enter the profession for which they have been training, at a *threshold* level. Everybody knows – the instructors on that same programme, the students themselves, the members of the profession or occupation in question – that there is still more to be learned, more experience needing to be gained, more skill and fluency to be acquired. On reflection, it seems obvious that even after initial professional qualification, more experience and learning is going to be necessary. This commitment to ongoing professional development is not unique to either the teaching profession more broadly, nor to teachers and trainers in further and adult education more specifically, although for the latter, a recognised route for CPD has been a long time coming and has suffered from a number of false starts. The requirement for compulsory CPD for all teachers in the sector that was mandated by the (now defunct) Institute for Learning was met with ambivalence at best by practitioners in the sector, leading as it did to too much CPD that was perceived as being top-down and management-led, lacking sufficient relevance to everyday practice (Orr, 2009). It seems right to say that a sector-led, ground-up approach would be more fruitful.

From CPD to JPD

The Society for Education and Training (SET – within which the ETF is located) also encourages CPD: trainers and teachers within the sector are encouraged to do so in order to remain in good professional standing (there is no longer any sense of 'maintaining a license to practice' attached to the discourses of CPD within the sector's professional body). The SET and ETF websites are noteworthy for their generosity in defining what counts as CPD, and suggest a range of formal and informal activities for maintaining and updating both pedagogical and subject-specific knowledge and skills. Much of this discourse is, unsurprisingly, framed around the ETF Professional Standards.

If we follow the ETF website links to the *Professional Standards Research Tool*, we find that one of the recommended approaches for maintaining and updating knowledge and practice is *Joint Practice Development* (JPD). Another link on the webpage leads to an adapted model of JPD that rather simplifies things (once again we have an example of an idea translated from place to place, and losing important detail as it does so), but if we go back to the source material, a richer model emerges.

The concept of JPD appears first in a research report from 2005 written by Michael Fielding and colleagues, all of whom worked either at the University of Sussex or for the Demos think tank, and funded by the Department for Education and Skills (as it then was). The research team – which included the above-mentioned Michael Eraut – was interested in exploring the ways in which groups of schools had, at that time, been set up to provide school-to-school professional development and training, modelling approaches that had made them successful so that other schools, perhaps in more social-deprived areas or that were seen as at risk of failing, might learn from these experiences and processes. From conducting research in over 30 different schools and 120 practitioners, Fielding et al. sought to account for the transfer of best practice – both between schools as institutions, and at an individual level. One of their key conclusions was that the development or improvement of practice was best accomplished in collaborative relationships, rather than if people were compelled to take part, and that a new term was needed to describe this process:

> Where teachers are developing new practices it is rare for them to replicate the good practice of others. In our fieldwork teachers were more likely to describe the extension and refinement of their existing repertoire of practices, through collaborative and affirming work with other teachers. Teachers saw themselves as having 'travelled' or 'grown' in their work. [...] This led us, in many cases, to question whether the joint work teachers were involved in should be labelled as 'practice transfer' or whether 'joint practice development' would provide a better description of their work. This is a move that validates the existing practice of teachers who are trying to learn new ways of working, and acknowledges the effort of those who are trying to support them, both in their having developed creative ways of working and the complex task of opening up and sharing practices with others.
>
> (Fielding et al., 2005: 32)

In 2012, a 'thinkpiece' written by David Hargreaves and published by the (now defunct) National College for School Leadership – one of a series of thinkpieces written by Hargreaves that outlined frameworks for enhancing education through encouraging 'self-improving' networks or partnerships of schools. Hargreaves does not refer to the Fielding et al. report in his paper, although his proposed definition of JPD is nonetheless similar in several ways:

Professional development becomes a continuous, pervasive process that builds craft knowledge, rather than an occasional activity that is sharply distinguished in time and space from routine classroom work. What we call this shift in professional development is important. [...] Joint practice development (JPD) is a term that captures the essential features of this form of professional development.

It is a **joint** activity, in which two or more people interact and influence one another, in contrast to the non-interactive, unilateral character of much conventional 'sharing good practice'.

It is an activity that focuses on teachers' professional **practice**, i.e. what they do, not merely what they know.

It is a **development** of the practice, not simply a transfer of it from one person or place to another, and so a form of school improvement.

(Hargreaves, 2012: 8–9, emphasis in the original).

What is joint practice development, therefore? Simply put, it is any kind of development activity that provides:

opportunities for the development of teachers' practice in such a way as to foreground the value of reciprocal conversations and relations;

changes or adjustments to pedagogy that are framed in terms of building on what is already practiced and known rather than on new approaches or replacement strategies;

spaces for discussion, coaching, and mentoring that do not have to be framed within formal, managerial processes such as observations of teaching, but that can emerge from peer-to-peer networks;

opportunities to adapt and try things out without a fear of failure, encouraging reflection and self-evaluation, but not causally tied to measurable outcomes such as improvements in learners' achievement rates.

From JPD to CoP

Over the past two decades (from the formation of the Institute for Learning in 2002, which, it has been argued, was responsible for a process of de-professionalisation within the sector rather than the other way round [Plowright and Barr, 2012]), we can argue that discourses around ongoing professional learning and development have, therefore, shifted away from a top-down model of CPD to a ground-up model of JPD. Models of CPD that are seen as requiring teachers and trainers to take part in training that they have little say over in terms of pace or content and that, having been evaluated, would appear to be of minimal impact in terms of ongoing professional learning, have been replaced with models of JPD that rest on collaboration, on partnerships within and across colleges, providing time and space for practitioners to access for themselves the professional conversations that they feel that they need, alongside more speculative and inquiry-based formal training events that aim to facilitate discussions rather than impose them. But what has this got to do with Communities of Practice?

There are several strands to answering this question. Firstly, as I hope that this book has been able to demonstrate, CoPs are a meaningful and valuable lens for exploring the ongoing learning of trainers and teachers as well as students and apprentices. Having established that a CoP is a social and cultural space where learning cannot help but happen, it follows that trajectories for learning – through participation – are available for all of the members of that community. Secondly, as we saw in Chapter 1, both the Education and Training Foundation and the Association for Learning Technology have organised events, conducted research, and produced publications that talk about Communities of Practice as ways to generate and share good practice, provide networks for professionals, and so forth. They may well be doing all of these things and more – but we cannot know because their use of CoP theory is insufficient and, consequently, the explanatory and predictive potential of CoP theory is difficult to apply. The theory deserves better. The third strand to this answer follows on from the first two. If my argument – that making proper use of CoP theory is a good thing to do – is to be taken seriously, then how can it be used to make sense of the emergence of JPD? Or, to put it another way, why would anyone need CoPs if they have JPD?

The answer to this question is simple: JPD is a framework for allowing us to think about our ongoing professional development as teachers and trainers, the important and necessary work that we do to remain in good standing, to refresh and update our subject specialist bodies of expertise and knowledge, and to extend and enhance our pedagogical practice. It is a label under which we can group together both how we go about these processes of ongoing learning, and a rationale for doing so in a particular way – the ground-up model of collaboration and ownership described above. What JPD does not do is *explain* how learning (of any kind, let alone what we might term 'ongoing professional learning' for the purposes of this discussion) happens, where it happens, or what structures and resources we need to ensure that it happens and why. This is a job for CoP theory. Joint practice development, therefore, needs to be considered as a *theoretical plug-in* (discussed in Chapter 2) to CoP theory if we are to maintain the overarching theoretical rationale presented in this book.

Plugging JPD into CoPs

As an overarching idea about how best to approach the stuff of ongoing professional development and learning, we can propose that the *idea* of JPD (how it is talked about or written about, how it is planned for, the tools and materials that are used to facilitate it, and so forth) be included within the **shared repertoire** of a Community of Practice. At the same time, the *doing* of JPD (the bringing together of people in different kinds of relationships on order to accomplish the work that they have set for themselves) can be seen as a form of **mutual engagement**. And, finally, the function and purpose of JPD (the engagement in a series of practices in order to bring about instances of ongoing professional learning and development) forms the **joint enterprise** of the community. So what kind of community is this? It is not a CoP such as a Community of Hairdressing Practice or a Community of Electrical Installation Practice, a tightly framed CoP centred around a specific vocation, profession or body of knowledge of the kind that we have discussed up to now. Instead, and remembering that even a single college is made up of a **constellation** of communities, we need to describe this JPD-focused practice as an additional CoP and then explain how it is aligned to the rest of the constellation.

In Chapters 1 and 2, we encountered the concept of the *dual professional*, a well-established idea within the sector that continues to provide a focus for the professional formation model that underpins the ETF professional standards. This is a concept that foregrounds the background of the teacher or trainer, recognising that many new entrants to the sector already possess considerable pools of experience, knowledge, and aptitude derived from their trade/vocational/professional experience and qualifications. At one level, therefore, the dual professionalism model can be seen as serving the interests of the sector workforce, allowing as it does the existing expertise of the individual teacher or trainer to be recognised and acknowledged. It also provides a space for the occupational expertise of the teacher to be sustained and enhanced in the future. Just as the workshops in a further education college ought to be equipped in order to meet current trade and industry specifications (after all, there is little point in having college students learn using outmoded tools and materials), so the teaching staff ought to maintain currency, to ensure that their knowledge, aptitude, and skills are up-to-date and reflect current, and not redundant, business or industry practices. Sustaining dual professionalism requires the teacher or trainer – and by extension their managers and employers – to build opportunities for relevant trade and industry updating and development, in addition to teacher education.

Interlude: critiques of dual professionalism

The argument against is that a model of dual professionalism serves to diminish the very teacher professionalism that ought to be encouraged through not only the completion of an initial professional qualification but also through subsequent continuing professional development. From this perspective, dual professionalism acts to take attention away from the professional ethos of the teacher that, in the further education sector is – arguably – already only weakly framed (and made weaker by the recent decision, at the time of writing, to reintroduce voluntarism into the education of teachers in the sector). For those commentators who seek to explore and inform an ethics or philosophy of teaching, it is by no means the case that the professional ethics of teaching are sufficiently closely related to those of many of the occupational areas represented in the further education curriculum, so that it can be assumed that they are straightforwardly transferable.

An empirical critique of dual professionalism can be found in the work of Bill Esmond and Hayley Wood. In their small-scale study of workshop-based tutors (they focussed on hospitality, construction, fabrication and welding, and motor vehicle tutors) they identified many instances of *subject mobility* (Esmond and Wood, 2017: 240) – tutors having to work across different subject areas, having either to acquire new bodies of skill quickly or refresh old skills that did not form part of their vocational specialism (rather like our fictional tutor in Chapter 6). Esmond and Wood's study is very small, based on interviews with six tutors, but the message is clear nonetheless. How can we develop and sustain dual professionalism if one half of that professionalism is prone to slippage or dilution, as tutors are pushed into working outside their specialisms?

Notwithstanding the critiques presented above, we might nonetheless imagine a Community of Dual Professional Practice (CoDPP: an ungainly label but it will do for now) that has continuing professional and/or occupational learning in order to facilitate the maintenance and development of dual professionalism. Within this CoDPP, joint practice development, as explored and defined above, forms one of the structuring resources: it informs all of the core components of the community – joint enterprise, mutual engagement, and shared repertoire. The doing and maintaining of dual professionalism is quite a vague, not to say elastic, notion, and as such this CoDPP must be *weakly framed* (in the manner defined by Boud and Middleton, 2003, and discussed in Chapter 3) because the practice of this community is varied and changeable, in comparison to a *tightly framed* CoP such as plumbing or veterinary nursing. We can plug JPD into this community of practice in the following ways:

1   JPD is a *joint* activity that rests on interaction and mutual influence between at least two people. This aligns to the *joint* enterprise of a CoP. The mutuality of JPD reflects the ways in which all members of a CoP engage in practice irrespective of their trajectory.
2   JPD rejects a close focus on teacher knowledge to the exclusion of that they do. JPD focuses on professional *practice*, which necessarily involves both knowing *and* doing, which in turn is characteristic of CoPs, which do not discriminate against so-called 'theoretical' or 'practical' bodies of knowledge and experience – ways of knowing are the same whether based around practices that involve manual activity or practices that involve mental activity, and are all of equal value.
3   JPD rests on the development of each teacher's professional practice on an individual basis, thereby leading to wider departmental or organisational shifts. It does not rely on the transfer of practice from place to place but focuses on site-specific practices. This focus on context and rejection of automatic transfer of practice is aligned to the rejection of the transfer of learning that is at the heart of social theories of learning and was critiqued by Jean Lave (1988) in particular (as discussed in Chapter 2).

However, there are some claims made for JPD that now need to be explained from a CoP perspective, notwithstanding the alignments discussed here.

Question: if JPD rejects the notion of transfer, then how do we actually develop our practice within our own professional contexts? How does what we do within the CoDPP make any difference to our occupational CoPs?

Answer: when participating in the CoDPP, the things that we discuss, the resources that we share, the techniques that we develop, and so forth all form part of our learning. Learning is a necessary aspect of membership and impacts on our **identities** (discussed in Chapter 1). When we travel back to our professional/occupational CoPs, what we have learned through the time spent in the CoDPP travels within and around us as a consequence of **multimembership** (discussed in Chapter 6). At the same time, any materials, routines, techniques or discourses that we have participated in and/or acquired when in the CoDPP can travel with us as **boundary objects** if they are not going to be absorbed into our professional CoPs. Otherwise, they can be adopted and adjusted in order to become part of the shared repertoire of our professional CoPs.

Question: engagement in our professional/occupational CoPs happens all of the time, but staff development events for JPD only happen occasionally, oftentimes with people from different colleges. What kind of CoPs are at work here?

Answer: the CoDPP does not have to meet on a specific or minimum number of occasions in order to accomplish the things that, as a CoP, it sets out to do. Practice need not be time-bound, fixed to a specific place, or require a certain number of community members, except insofar as the practice of the community – the stuff that the community does and the way that it does it – requires. Whether or not a CoP is weakly framed or strongly framed does not depend on the mode of attendance (CoPs can be blended or even virtual – see below) or the frequency of gathering, but simply on the cohesion – or flexibility – of the practices being engaged with. Nor does a CoP only have to draw members from other communities within the adjacent constellation.

Question: finding time for professional development is difficult: can online-only activities work equally well?

Answer: there is no reason why not, all things being equal. But it is important to remember to think about the spaces and places that are being formed and utilised. Not every meeting of people is a community of practice; nor is it the case that everything labelled as being a CoP really *is* one – we have to do some thinking, reading, and research in order to establish our claims to being on a trajectory within a CoP. The same applies for virtual or online communities of practice (Bond and Lockee, 2014). Whether a community gathers in a physical place or virtual space is irrelevant and makes no difference in terms of CoP theory. So long as the key elements of joint enterprise, shared repertoire, and mutual engagement are identifiable, then a CoP is always going to be present. Like any other CoP, we just need to know what we are looking for: we need to be sufficiently familiar with CoP theory to inform both our inquiry and our action.

Final conclusions (1)

Communities of Practice in further and adult education: constellations, teachers, and students

When we talk about the further and adult education sector, what we are actually talking about is an overarching constellation of communities of practice that are interested in things to do with the teaching and assessment of professional, technical, and vocational curricula to a range of students – from 16 year-olds to adult returners. These communities of practice have come together in colleges or other institutional forms such as community education centres, shaped into organisational structures by long-standing traditions as to how best formal education should be arranged, kept in place by successive policies and funding regimes as well as accepted cultures and habits. We might imagine that these constellations, if not some of the CoPs within them, cross international borders through events such as the WorldSkills competition (https://worldskills.org/what/competitions/), but this might make our mental image of all of the CoPs involved difficult to keep hold of.

This sector-wide constellation is made up of a number of sub-constellations, each centred on an institution: or, to put it another way, we might imagine an individual college or other organisation as consisting of a constellation, made up of a number of CoPs. Most of these communities are centred around the teaching and assessment of specific occupational or professional bodies of expertise that are commonly referred to as departments, curriculum areas, or subject areas. Some of these are centred around other specific bodies of work that are equally part of the overall work of the college as an entity, but which are not directly centred on subject expertise and pedagogic practice (for example, college finance departments): these fall outside the scope of our current inquiry. Within a college there may be other groups or collectives of people at work together or sharing resources and so forth. These may also be CoPs – but they may not be. A 'community of practice' is not synonymous with a 'group of colleagues'.

The different Communities of Pedagogic Practice that are found within a college constellation are to be understood as social and cultural spaces and places within which both teachers and students work: the focus of their work is the doing of the subject specialism that the CoP is about. Teachers and students, in other words, have as their shared practice the doing of the curriculum – the teaching, the learning, the assessment. The different relationships to the curriculum that the teachers and student have is explained in terms of their different trajectories and their standpoints as members. Students will only ever be peripheral and temporary members, passing through these pedagogic CoPs as a necessary precursor to membership of a professional or occupational CoP. Teachers are full members, but may also still be members of professional or occupational CoPs as well. And of course, both students and teachers may be members of other CoPs that have nothing to do with further and adult education.

Being in a CoP necessarily entails learning: learning is an unavoidable consequence of participation, whatever trajectory someone is on. For the student, the learning is centred on the occupational or professional expertise that is at the heart of the joint enterprise of the practice. But they may also learn other things as a consequence of being in a community that is part of a constellation: other aspects of 'being a student in further/adult education' may also be learned (through multimembership). For the teacher, learning is centred on the practices of teaching and assessment. Through maintaining connections with the profession or trade, teachers may learn new thing that enhance or grow their expertise as subject specialists.

Multimembership works in different ways, therefore. For teachers, multimembership is central to their ongoing status as dual professionals. Their multimembership of *at least* one pedagogical CoP (teachers may sometimes work in two institutions, or teach in two programme areas), of their subject specialist CoP, and, if available, a professional development CoP, provides the *nexus of practices* through which their professional identities are established and nourished. For students, multimembership may be present in the relationship between time spent at college and time spent in the workplace – on placement or day release, as well as in relationships between their programme of study and any other CoPs within the college constellation that they are engaged with.

The lines of communication that exist between the CoPs within the college constellation, and between different college constellations, allow ways of knowing, bodies of expertise and experience, materials, resources and people to travel across the sector as a whole and to learn from these other communities and constellations in different ways.

Outside the college constellations are other CoPs that are not directly concerned with the *practices* of teaching and learning in the same way that the teachers and students are. Awarding bodies, employer organisations and professional bodies are of course central participants in their own right, but their practice is qualitatively different from that which takes place within the college-based communities. These CoPs have things to say about bodies of expertise and knowledge that travel to the college constellations in the form of boundary objects such as curriculum documentation, accompanied by brokers such as external verifiers.

Therefore, when we talk about the further and adult education sector as a whole, we are talking about an overarching constellation that weaves around a number of other constellations – colleges – that in themselves are constituted of multiple communities of practice. Alongside the college constellations we can imagine awarding body constellations and professional body constellations, in turn made up of other CoPs – specific examination boards, specific employers, skills councils, and so forth. Relations between all of these are managed through a constant processes of brokerage and the transport of boundary objects.

Final conclusions (2)

What does knowing about CoPs help us to do?

When we see the further and adult education sector in terms of constellations and communities – some long-standing and others brought about through setting up learning architectures – it shifts our perspective. This is not a radical or disturbing shift; rather, it is a shift in emphasis, a way of focusing attention onto several factors that are of importance to the sector and to the students and teachers in it. Some of these are noticed for the first time, others take on a new level of importance, and others are recognised from a new standpoint. Things that were taken-for-granted become more explicit, and other things that were hard to explain or justify become easier to talk about.

A CoP perspective foregrounds the importance of authenticity. This relates to several things. Firstly, it relates to the expertise and experience of the teacher, who needs to be an authentic representation of her or his subject specialist CoPs. This authenticity, an aspect of identity, is an important element of a successful pedagogy within a CoP because the apprenticeship model relies on the 'expert other'. Instead of subscribing to a facilitator model that somehow depicts the teacher as being 'equal' to the students, teachers instead should take pride in their ownership of their expertise. Teachers and students are not the same or equal from the point of view of the practice of that community (whilst in other CoPs, the position may be reversed): their different identities and trajectories signify the different positions that they occupy.

It is this authenticity through expertise that informs pedagogy, including assessment, which is specific to the CoP. How one body of specialist competence and knowledge is exercised, embodied, talked about, and written about is always different to any other. Some do have similarities and are closely aligned, whilst others are not. The extent to which the practices or repertoire from one CoP might usefully be imported or exported to another is best judged by the teachers – the full participants – within the CoPs in question. Authentic learning requires authentic pedagogy, and valid and reliable assessment similarly requires authentic expertise.

Not everything in a CoP can be written down in an explicit manner: some forms of knowing or of expertise defy explanation. Others are not always discernible to visitors or brokers. People outside a subject specific CoP who nonetheless ae capable of influencing what happens within that community need to engage in a genuine dialogue with the representatives of that community in order for these hard-to-see practices to be taken account of.

Likewise, it is not possible to directly see learning happen. Changes in practice – a new aptitude to the completion of a specific task, or a new confidence in explaining a problem – are the result of learning, not the learning itself. What the process of learning might look like is difficult if not impossible to specify, although what can be stated with more confidence is what an environment for the opportunity for authentic learning might look like. Simply put, the required environments for authentic learning are those that contain sufficient structuring resources of the learning architecture – people and things. Students will not be able to progress along their planned and/or desired trajectories if these resources are not made available: without them, the participation of the students will not be authentic and therefore will not be legitimate.

Learning is not a process that can be neatly switched on or off. There is no 'passive' as distinct from 'active' learning. Learning happens all of the time, in ways that cannot always be measured easily.

Teaching is just one among the many structuring resources that can be included within a learning architecture if the ambition is to establish a new CoP. Alternatively, teaching can be found as one element amongst the shared repertoire of any other CoP within a college constellation. What teaching looks like is highly situated – that is to say, it is highly context-dependent. Describing teaching in terms of being 'good' or 'outstanding' is misleading: only someone who also shares the same authentic practices of the community will be able to recognise the teaching that is right for that community – that belongs within the shared repertoire of the community. CoPS that are aligned to each other will share aspects of their repertoire – including teaching – across their boundaries, but a degree of reworking or customisation will always be required.

If we think that something is not quite right in our teaching, with our assessments, or from the perspective of our students, then our starting point should always be to consider the condition of the CoP, including the trajectories and identities of our students, the structuring resources (our pedagogies, our tools and artefacts, and so forth), the legitimacy of students' peripheral participation, and so forth. One element is not more important than the other in maintaining the practice of the community.

And to finish ...

We might begin our inquiries into communities of practice in further and adult education with something very mundane, such as a PDF of a unit from an Extended Diploma (it doesn't matter which one). From this starting point, we can track the journey that the PDF took before it arrived in our staff room – or on a screen in a workshop or classroom, being explained to the students. We can follow the unit back to the qualification that it comes from, then to the curriculum that it belongs to, then to the employer body that advised on the course content. We can then track the PDF in the other direction, looking at how it is made sense of by the tutors, and whether it makes sense by itself or whether it needs someone else to interpret it. We can look at how it shapes an instance of pedagogic practice, how it shapes lesson and course planning, and how it steers the students to particular kinds of practical and/or written work. In this way, we can trace the trajectories of the different participants involved, the outlines and locations of the CoPs involved, the instances of boundary crossing and brokerage that were needed to help the PDF to travel to where it needs to be, and the discourses and actions that it leaves behind. And this can all start with just one unit from just one diploma! Imagine the trajectories, members, communities, brokers and artefacts that we would have to describe for just one curriculum area, and then one college, and then a regional college network, and then …

References

Barton, D. and Tusting, K. (eds.) (2005) *Beyond Communities of Practice: Language, Power and Social Context.* Cambridge: Cambridge University Press.

Black, P. and Wiliam, D. (1998a) *Inside the Black Box: Raising Standards Through Classroom Assessment.* London: GL Assessment.

Black, P. and Wiliam, D. (1998b) Assessment and classroom learning. *Assessment in Education* 5 (1) 7–71. doi:10.1080/0969595980050102.

Bond, M. and Lockee, B. (2014) *Building virtual communities of practice for distance educators.* London: Springer.

Boud, D. and Middleton, H. (2003) Learning from others at work: communities of practice and informal learning. *Journal of Workplace Learning* 15 (5) 194–202. doi:10.1108/13665620310483895.

Eraut, M. (1994) *Developing Professional Knowledge and Competence.* Abingdon: RoutledgeFalmer.

Esmond, B. and Wood, H. (2017) More morphostasis than morphogenesis? The 'dual professionalism' of English further education workshop tutors. *Journal of Vocational Education and Training* 69 (2) 229–245. doi:10.1080/13636820.2017.1309568.

Fielding, M., Bragg, S., Craig, J., Cunningham, I., Eraut, M., Gillinson, S., Horne, M., Robinson, C., and Thorp, J. (2005) *Factors influencing the transfer of good practice.* Nottingham: Department for Education and Skills.

Hargreaves, D.H. (2012) *A self-improving school system: towards maturity.* Nottingham: Department for Education.

Hughes, J. (2007) Lost in translation: communities of practice – the journey from academic model to practitioner tool. In Hughes, J., Jewson, N., and Unwin, L. (eds.) *Communities of Practice: critical perspectives.* London: Routledge. 30–40.

Lave, J. (1988) *Cognition in Practice: Mind, Mathematics and Culture in Everyday Life.* Cambridge: Cambridge University Press.

Lea, M. (2005) 'Communities of practice' in higher education: useful heuristic or educational model? In Barton, D. and Tusting, K. (eds.) *Beyond Communities of Practice: Language, Power and Social Context.* Cambridge: Cambridge University Press. 180–197.

Orr, K. (2009) Performativity and professional development: the gap between policy and practice in the English further education sector. *Research in Post Compulsory Education* 14 (4) 479–489. doi:10.1080/13596740903361016.

Plowright, D. and Barr, G. (2012) An integrated professionalism in further education: a time for phronesis? *Journal of Further and Higher Education* 36 (1) 1–16. doi:10.1080/0309877X.2011.590584.

Wenger, E., McDermott, R. and Snyder, W. (2002) *Cultivating Communities of Practice.* Boston: Harvard Business School Press.

Index

9781032180335